全 国 科 普 创 作 与 产 品 研 发 示 范 团 队 作 品

快乐学堂系列

距离课堂最近的权威读物
影响孩子一生的阅读经典

语言中的乐趣

刘兴诗 黄寰 / 主编

青少年百科图书馆

科学性 趣味性 文学性

父 母 送 给 孩 子 最 好 的 人 生 礼 物

培养学习兴趣，提高综合素质，养成良好习惯，
探究人生道理，训练思维能力。

时代出版传媒股份有限公司
安 徽 教 育 出 版 社

图书在版编目（CIP）数据

语言中的乐趣 / 刘兴诗，黄寰主编．—合肥：安徽教育出版社，2015

（青少年百科图书馆）

ISBN 978-7-5336-8071-8

Ⅰ．①语…　Ⅱ．①刘…②黄…　Ⅲ．①英语 - 青少年读物　Ⅳ．①H319.4

中国版本图书馆 CIP 数据核字（2015）第 203513 号

语言中的乐趣

YUYAN ZHONG DE LEQU

出 版 人：郑　可
质量总监：姚　莉
策划编辑：胡延东　杨多文　徐宝妹
责任编辑：徐宝妹
装帧设计：戴　军
责任印制：王　琳
出版发行：时代出版传媒股份有限公司　安徽教育出版社
地　　址：合肥市经开区繁华大道西路 398 号　邮编：230601
网　　址：http：//www.ahep.com.cn
营销电话：（0551）63683011，63683013
排　　版：北京名壹堂图书有限公司
印　　刷：三河市腾飞印务有限公司
开　　本：660mm × 960mm　1/16
印　　张：12.5
字　　数：174 千字
版　　次：2017 年 3 月第 1 版　2017 年 3 月第 1 次印刷
定　　价：29.80 元

序言

我们从呱呱坠地开始，就与这个浩瀚的宇宙有了质的接触，在与这个万花筒似的世界建立密切关系的过程中，我们会发现各种有趣的事物，接收到不同学科的知识。随着人类科技的发展，广阔飘渺的宇宙俨然成了一本供世人阅读的活页大百科全书，等待人们去探索，去学习，去掌握，去开拓。“青少年百科图书馆”丛书力求贯彻国家课程标准和各项专题教育纲要的精神，内容深入浅出，集知识性、趣味性、文学性为一体，以诙谐有趣的口吻、简洁规范的文字、精美生动的插图为读者呈现科普知识的饕餮大餐，这些科普知识与中小学各学科内容紧密结合，有助于提高中小学生的科学素养和人文素养。

本丛书内容丰富，有趣味盎然的古老传说、文笔优美的名人轶事、引人入胜的科学小实验、简明的知识等。为了让读者能够轻松地阅读，快乐地学习，积极地思考，丛书的每一篇文章都有紧扣课程标准的“知识点”、开拓视野的“知识链接”、培养探索能力的“动动手”以及扣人心弦的手绘插图四个部分，让读者在循序渐进的阅读过程中与科普进行深层次的精神交流，同时激发读者对科普的热情，培养读者对科普的兴趣。

本丛书共计 19 本，取材广泛，知识新颖，分为两个系列：“快乐学堂系列”“求知阶梯系列”，文字累计超过 300 万字。“快乐学堂系列”有 10 本，读完这一系列读物，将有助于你拥有健康的心灵（心理健康教育），理解诚信的真谛（诚信教育），具备初步的法律意识（法律），了解安全自救的基本知识（安全教育），增强对中国文化的美好情感（语文），懂得生命在于运动（体育），务实英文学习基础（英语），树立环保意识（环境教育），养成懂礼貌的好习惯（礼仪教育），展开科学之旅（科学）。“求知阶梯系列”有9本书，读完这一系列读物，你可以学习交谈的艺术（礼仪教育），爱上诚信这个朋友（诚信教育），体会弹指一挥间的快乐（体育），找到快乐的源泉（心理健康教育），接触生态建筑（生物），进入立体世界（数学），触摸穿越时空的门（物理），感受世界各地的魅力（英语），找准自己的目标（思想品德）。

在中国科协项目、四川省科技计划科普培训项目、四川省科协项目和成都市科协项目等的支持下，来自全国科普创作与产品研发示范团队“成都理工大学刘兴诗工作室”、成都理工大学四川省哲学社会科学普及基地、成都理工大学大学生记者站、四川创新区域经济研究院、四川省科普作协、成都市科普作协等部门众多一线教学工作者和有着丰富写作经验的科普作者经过两年多的精心策划和编纂，“青少年百科图书馆”系列图书终于与读者见面了。同时，丛书的所有绘图也得到了成都崇州市艺林美术学校支持，由其组织供稿。作者团队殚精竭虑，在参考众多文献的基础上，尽量使丛书反映出当代科学发展的最新信息，但是由于精力和水平有限，书中难免出现些许瑕疵，望读者不吝赐教，以便我们不断改进。

刘兴诗

2016年7月

目 录

第8章 Chicken Soup心灵鸡汤 / 165

第1章

School Life

五彩校园

School Life in Foreign Countries
国外的校园生活

知识点 To know about school life in foreign countries
了解国外小学生活

Textbooks in USA Schools

Schools in the USA do not have a specific teaching plan for teachers to follow, and they do not have the same textbooks for all the children to use around a state or the country. Teachers have to decide what books they would use and what they would teach in their classes. Yet some schools would also provide textbooks for the students, and the teachers would often encourage students to find mistakes and wrong points in the book. Teaching like this has many advantages. Teachers can bring out what they are good at. Students may be more interested in what they are studying, and can develop better in critical thinking. But at the same time, teaching like this may bring trouble to the next teacher. He has to spend some time in finding out what the students have learned before he begins his

teaching.

[**Notes 注释**]

Words

specific adj. 特定的
textbook n. 教科书，课本
encourage v. 鼓励
advantage n. 优点
critical thinking n. 批判性思维
at the same time 同时

Sentence

He has to spend some time in finding out what the students have learned before he begins his teaching. 在开始自己的教学之前，他不得不花些时间了解学生已经掌握了哪些知识。“spend time in doing sth.” 意思是“花费时间做某事”，in 可以省略。例如：我做家庭作业花了两个小时。可以说“I spend two hours in doing my homework”也可以说“I spend two hours doing my homework.”

[文章大意]

美国的教科书

美国的学校通常没有特定的教学计划，也没有一个全州或全国统一的教材，老师自己决定用什么教材和教什么内容。当然也有学校提供教材，老师通常就会鼓励学生找出书中的错误。这种教学方式有很多好处。老师可以教他们最擅长的东西，学生对所学知识会更感兴趣。在学习过程中，学生的批判思维能得到更好的训练。但这种方式也会给

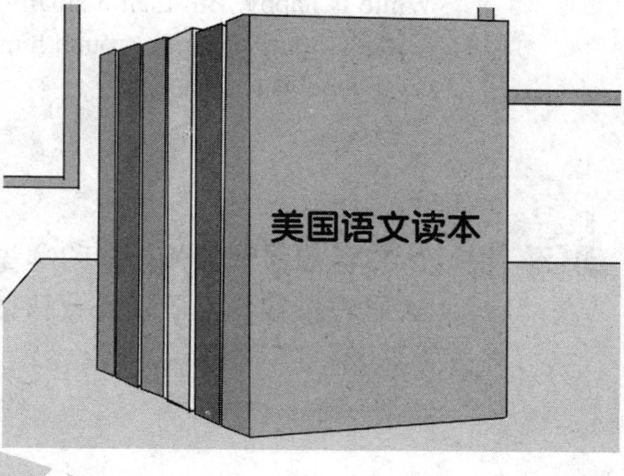

下任老师带来麻烦，那就是在开始自己的教学之前，他不得不花些时间了解学生已经掌握了哪些知识。

知识链接

英国的小学一个学年通常有三个学期（term）。从九月初到十二月中，是一个学年的第一学期，也叫秋季学期。第二学期（即春季学期）从一月初到复活节（通常在四月的某个周末）。从复活节结束到七月中，是一个学年的最后一学期，也称夏季学期。

扩展阅读

Don't Cry

Mr. White is a teacher. He lives not far from the school, so he always walks to the school in the morning.

Mr. White walks to school on a very cold and windy morning in November. The cold wind goes into his eyes, and tears began running out. He reaches the school, opens the door and goes into the classroom. It is nice and warm there and Mr. White is happy. But then a small boy looks at him for a few seconds, puts his arms around him and says kindly, "Don't cry. School isn't that bad."

动动手

1. 你还想了解国外小学的哪些方面呢？自己去查一查吧！
2. 思考：你认为学校统一教材好还是老师自己选教材好？

School Test in England
英国的考试

知识点 To know about test in England
了解英国的考试

School Report

NAME：MARY

SUBJECTS：

Mathematics

She is not so good at this，but she has tried her best to catch up with others.

French

Her reading is very good，and she can remember many words.

第1章 五彩校园

Physics

She is a little weak in this，but has done better than before.

Chemistry

She can work out many difficulties. Well done.

English

She's got the best score in the class. Keep it up.

Geography

She is familiar（熟悉）with the names of many places in the world.

History

She likes reading stories about women.

Art

She can draw pictures like real ones.

Music

She does not like pop songs，though sings very well. Why?

Physical Education（P. E.）

She needs more outdoor exercise.

TEACHER：HELEN

[**Notes 注释**]

Words

subject n. 学科　mathematics n. 数学　physics n. 物理

chemistry n. 化学　geography n. 地理　art n. 艺术

physical education（P.E.）n. 体育　draw picture v. 画画

outdoor exercise n. 室外活动

Sentence

She is not so good at this，but she has tried her best to catch up with others. 她不太擅长数学，但已尽力追赶其他同学。"be good at…" 表示"擅长做……"，例如：If you expect to study in the US，you must be good at English. 如果你期望到美国念书，英文必须要好！"try one's best to do sth. ” 意思是“尽力去做某件事情”，例如：One should try one’s best to help others. 一个人应该尽力帮助他人。“catch up with sth.” 意为“赶上、追上”，例如：I'll catch up with you，okay? 我一会儿赶上你，好吗?

[文章大意]

成绩报告单

姓名：玛丽

科目：数学，不太擅长，但非常努力。

法语，阅读很棒，记了很多单词

物理，有点弱，但有进步。

化学，能解许多难题，很好！

英语，考了班上的第一，继续加油！

地理，熟悉世界上的很多地名。

历史，喜欢读有关女性的故事。

美术，画出的画像真的一样。

音乐，虽然唱得很好，但不喜欢流行音乐，为什么？

体育，需要多参加户外体育活动。

老师签名：海伦

知识链接

11+ 考试：在英国，许多小学生在最后一年都会参加一次统考。由于参考学生大多数都是十一二岁，这次考试就得名“11+ 考试”。如果考试成绩优秀，学生就可以升入相当于中国重点中学的文法学校学习。其余的学生进入现代中学就读。

扩展阅读

A Dollar per Point

One day，a teacher was giving a big test to his students. He handed out（分发）all of the test paper and went back to his desk to wait.

Once the test was over，the students all handed the test paper back in. The teacher noticed that one of the students had attached（附上）a $100 bill to his paper with a note saying，“a dollar per point.”

The next class the teacher handed the test paper back out. This student got back his paper and also $64 changes.

动动手

1. 按照文中的成绩单格式制作一份自己的成绩单吧。
2. 思考：你发现中外学生成绩单的区别有哪些？

Language Learning
学语言

知识点 To know how to learn language well
怎么学好语言

Don't Be Afraid of Making Mistakes

The best way to learn a language is to use it. The best way of learning English is to talk in English as much as possible. Sometimes you will get your words mixed up and people will not understand you. Sometimes people will say things too quickly and you won't understand them. But if you keep your sense of humor, you can always have a good laugh at the mistakes you make. Don't be sad if people seem to laugh at your mistakes. It's much better for people to laugh at your mistakes than to be angry because they don't understand what you are saying.

The most important rule for learning English is "Don't be afraid of making mistakes because everyone makes mistakes."

[**Notes 注释**]

Words

language n. 语言　　　mas much as possible 尽可能多

mix up 混合　　　sense of humor 幽默感

mistake n. 错误　　be afraid of 害怕

Sentence

Don't be unhappy if people seem to laugh at your mistakes. 如果你发觉有人笑话你的语言错误，别不高兴！"laugh at"为固定搭配，意思是"笑话；嘲笑"，对象通常为人，如 I am so sad because all of them are laughing at me. 他们所有人都嘲笑我，我觉得非常悲伤。

It's much better for people to laugh at your mistakes than to be angry because they don't understand what you are saying. 笑你总比不知道你在讲什么而生气好吧。"It is much better to do…"，意思是"做……要好得多"，如 It is much better to be healthy than to be in a good shape. 健康的身体比好身材要重要得多。类似表达还有"…would better to do…"，意思是"……最好……"。

[**文章大意**]

不要害怕犯错

学语言最好的方法就是多用，所以要学好英语就要尽可能多地用英语交谈。有时你可能会混淆了单词，人们听不懂你说的是什么；有时可能人们讲得太快，你听不懂他们在说什么。但是只要你有幽默感，你就会发现自己犯的错误有多可笑。如果你发觉有人笑话你的语言错误，别不高兴！笑你总比不知道你在讲什么而生气好吧？因此学英语的重要原则就是：不要怕犯错误，因为每个人都会犯错误！

知识链接

联合国官方语言共六种，包括阿拉伯语（Arabic）、汉语、英语、法语（French）、俄语（Russian）、和西班牙语（Spanish）。联合国的所有会议和官方文件都会使用这些语言。

扩展阅读

But They Have Trouble

Dick is a teacher. He usually went to France or Germany for a few weeks during his holiday, and he speaks French and German quite well.

One year Dick planned to go to Greece. He said to one of his friends, "I' m going to have a holiday in Athens. But I don' t speak Greek, so I'll go to evening classes and have Greek lessons for a month before I go."

He studied very hard for a month and then his holiday began.

When he came back a few weeks later, his friend asked, "Did you have any trouble with your Greek when you were in Athens, Dick?"

"No, I didn' t have any trouble." Answered Dick, "but the Greeks did."

动动手

1. 全世界共有多少种语言？查一查吧！
2. 思考：在学习语言的过程中，你会怎样提高自己的交流水平？

A Math Problem
数学问题

知识点 To know about numbers
了解有关数字的知识

A Math Problem

One day on his way to school, Bill passed a fruit shop. There was a sign on the window. It said, "Apples—five cents for six apples." An idea came to Bill and he went into the shop.

"How much are the apples?" he asked the shopkeeper.

"Five cents for six apples."

"But I don't want six apples."

"How many apples do you want?"

"It is not a question of how many apples I want. It is a problem in math."

"What do you mean by a problem in math?" asked the man.

"Well, if six apples are worth five cents, then five apples are worth four cents, four apples are worth three cents, three apples are worth two cents, two apples are worth one cent and one apple is worth nothing. I only want one apple, and if one apple is worth nothing, then I will not pay you."

Bill picked out a good apple, began to eat it, and walked happily out of the shop. The man looked at him with surprise and could not say a word.

[**Notes 注释**]

Words

sign n. 标志；招牌　　cent n. 美分

shopkeeper n. 商店老板；店主　　worth adj. 值（多少）钱的

on one's way to (some place) 到……去的路上

Sentences

It said, "Apples—five cents for six apples." 它（招牌）上面写着："苹果——五美分六个。"此句中的"said"为say的过去式形式，通常与表示物体的词连用，意为"指示、显示、表明"等，如：The clock says half past two. 时钟显示现在两点半。

I only want one apple, and if one apple is worth nothing, then I will not pay you. 我只要一个苹果，既然一个苹果不要钱，我就不付你钱了。"Worth"是形容词，表示"价值（多少）钱"，通常用在be动词后面，其后接名词、代词、数词或动词的-ing形式。如：The painting is worth thousands of dollars. 这幅画值几千美元。The film is worth seeing. 这部电影值得一看。

[**文章大意**]

一道数学题

一天，比尔在上学的路上看到一家水果店的招牌写着："苹果——五美分六个。"比尔心生一计，走进店里对老板说："如果六个苹果五美分，那么五个苹果就是四美分，四个苹果三美分，三个苹果两美分，两个苹果一美分，一个苹果就不要钱。我只要一个苹果，既然一个苹果

不要钱，我就不付你钱了。”比尔挑了一个大苹果开始吃了起来，然后高高兴兴地走出了店门。店主吃惊地看着比尔，一句话也说不出来。

知识链接

我们今天所用的数字，即1、2、3、4、5、6、7、8、9和0，被称为阿拉伯数字。事实上，他们最初是由印度人发明的，大约在公元8世纪传入阿拉伯地区。后来阿拉伯人把这些数字传入欧洲各国以及全世界，所以得名阿拉伯数字。

扩展阅读

Unlucky Number—13

Many people don't think that the number 13 is a lucky number. Many hotels do not have a 13th floor. The floors just go directly from 12 to 14，and there is no number13. Some people will never sit at a table with 12 other people. Why is 13 an unlucky number?

According to the Christian religion（基督教），Judas（犹大）was the 13th person at Jesus Christ's（耶稣）last supper. And it was he who betrayed（背叛）Jesus. So now many people consider it very unlucky to have 13 people around a dinner table. They believe that if 13 people sit down to have dinner together, one of them would die within the year.

In fact，there are no lucky or unlucky numbers；they exist only in our heads—or in the heads of some of us—and they might become lucky or unlucky only if we make them as such.

动动手

1. 你能用英语从1数到1000吗？试一试吧！
2. 思考：中国人认为那些数字不吉利？为什么？

Stationery
文具

知识点 To know different stationeries
了解不同文具

Chinese Brush

Chinese brush is one kind of the Chinese traditional writing tools. It is also a traditional painting tool. It is made of animal hairs, so it gets its name.

It is said that Chinese brush was invented by Meng Tian in the Qin Dynasty. So it has a history of more than 2,000 years. The Chinese brush

has made great contributions to the great culture of China and to promote inter-cultural communications between different countries in the world. The Chinese brush is a treasure for the world and though pencils, pens or other tools are popular, yet none can replace the Chinese brush. Do you know how to choose a good Chinese brush? Qualities of a good Chinese brush include:

The brush tip is pointed;

The hair should have the same length;

There is enough hair in the tip;

The hair is soft.

[**Notes 注释**]

Words

Chinese brush n. 毛笔　　traditional adj. 传统的

inter-cultural adj. 跨文化的　　replace v. 替代 quality n. 质量

is made of…由……制成（能看出原料）

make great contributions to…对……做出巨大的贡献

Sentences

It is said that Chinese brush was invented by Meng Tian in the Qin Dynasty. 据传毛笔是秦朝大臣蒙恬发明的。“It is said that…”意思是“据说……”，它可以变为：People say that…或“从句的主语 +be said to do”，例如，“据说未来很美丽”可以翻译为“It is said that future is very beautiful”或“People say that future is very beautiful”或“Future is said to be very beautiful”.

It is made of animal hairs, so it gets its name. 毛笔是用动物的毛制成，所以称为“毛笔”。“be made of…”意思是“由……制成（能看出原料）”，和它相似的表达是 be made from，两者都是“由什么制成”的意思，但 be made of 是可以看出原材料的，例如：The sweater was made of wool. 毛衣是羊毛做的（可以看出的）；be made from 是看不出原材料的，例如：The paper is made from wood. 纸是树木做的（看不出来的）。

[文章大意]

毛笔

毛笔是中国的传统书写工具和绘画工具。毛笔是用动物的毛制成，所以称为“毛笔”。据传毛笔是秦朝大臣蒙恬发明的，距今已有2000多年的历史。几千年来，它为创造中华民族光辉灿烂的文化，为促进汉民族与世界各族的文化交流，做出了卓越的贡献。好的毛笔具有以下特征：

1. 毛笔顶端要尖锐；
2. 毛笔毫毛要齐平；
3. 毛笔毫毛要充足；
4. 毛笔毫毛要柔软。

知识链接

小朋友们每天都要和各种文具打交道。数学课上会用到：尺子、铅笔、计算器（calculator）、圆规（compass）、三角板（set square）、橡皮擦、草稿本等等；语文课上会用到：钢笔、课本、字典（dictionary）、墨水（ink）等等；自然课上还需要地球仪（globe），美术课上还需要蜡笔（crayon）；老师上课的时候需要用到的有：粉笔（chalk）、黑板等等。

扩展阅读

They Are All Proud of Themselves

Ruler：I do things directly（直接地），and I can control（控制）myself very well.

Bag：I experience the study pressure of the students.

Pen：I am very outspoken（直言的）and there is much ink（墨水）in me. People can remember me easily.

Rubber：I have a thick skin but I am not afraid to make mistakes（错误），and I can correct（改正）my mistakes fast.

Bookshelf：I live with books all my life and I am already a "scholar"（书生）.

动动手

1. 你还能说出其他什么文具么？
2. 思考：在电脑广泛使用的今天，有专家呼吁在中小学开设毛笔课，你赞同吗？

Reading Selectively
有选择地阅读

知识点 To know how to choose good books to read
了解如何选择有益的书

Books

As well known，books teach us to learn life，truth，science and many other useful things. They increase our knowledge，broaden our minds and strengthen our character. In other words，they are our good teachers and wise friends. This is the reason why our parents always encourage us to read more books.

Reading is a good thing，but we must pay great attention to the choice

of books. It is true that we can learn from good books. However，bad books will do us more harm than good.

【Notes 注释】

Words

increase v. 增加　　broaden v. 加宽　　strengthen v. 加强

character n. 品格　　encourage v. 鼓励　　pay attention to 注意

Sentence

This is the reason why our parents always encourage us to read more books. 这是为什么我们的父母总是鼓励我们要多读书。“This is the reason why...”这个句型表示“这就是为什么……”，this 也可换成 that 或 it。如 That was the reason why I missed the class. 那就是为什么我没有去上学。本句中“encourage”表示“鼓励”，常用的搭配为 encourage sb. to do sth. 鼓励某人去干某事。如：Our teachers always encourage us to express ourselves in class. 老师总是鼓励我们要勇于在课堂上表达自己的观点。

[文章大意]

书籍

众所周知，书籍教我们学习人生、真理、科学以及其他许多有用的东西。它们能丰富我们的知识，开阔我们的视野并改善我们的品格。换句话说，它们是我们的良师益友。这是为什么我们的父母总是鼓励我们要多读书。

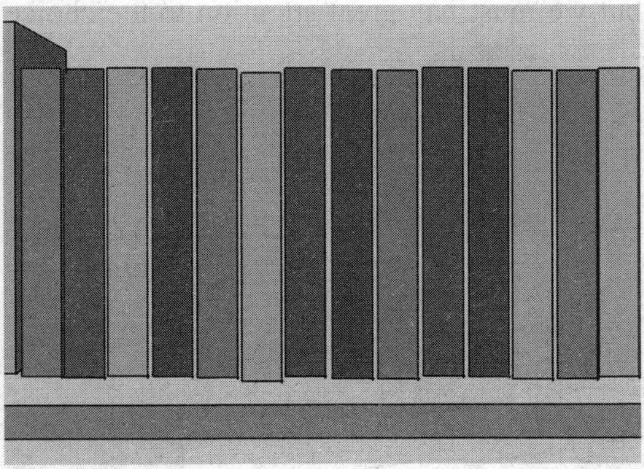

读书是好事，但我们必须注意书的选择。我们能从好书中获得益处。然而，坏书却对我们有害无益。

知识链接

国际儿童读物联盟（The International Board on Books for Young People，简称 IBBY）是 1953 年在苏黎世成立的一个非营利组织，旨在促进儿童更多地阅读。它规定安徒生的生日也就是 4 月 2 日为国际儿童读书日（International Children's Book Day），每年确定一个主题，在世界儿童中开展读书活动。

扩展阅读

Can You Read?

John lives in the countryside. One day he goes to the town. He goes into a restaurant and sits down at a table. When he looks around, he sees many old people put eyeglasses on before reading their newspaper, so after lunch he goes to buy some glasses.

The man in the shop lets him try on a lot of glasses, but John always says, "No, I can't read with these."

The man is more and more surprised. He says, "Excuse me, but can you read?"

"No, of course I can't!" John says, "That's why I want to buy glasses. I think they can help me read."

动动手

1. 给同学介绍你最喜欢的一本书。
2. 思考：你怎么看"开卷有益"这个说法？

School Regulations
校规

知识点 To know regulations for American and Chinese pupils
了解中美不同的学生守则

School Regulations in USA

Every school has its own regulations to tell the students what they can or cannot do at school. The regulations may be different for different schools, but many are the same. For example, many schools in USA may ask you to come to school on time and finish all work by yourself. And of course, you cannot cheat when taking a test. But if you have difficulty in class, you can make an appointment with your teacher. He or she will be glad to help you. Some schools have specific regulations for asking for a leave. You must bring a note from your parents when you are absent. And the only excuse you may have to be absent from school is that when you are sick, family members pass away or when it is a religious holiday.

[Notes 注释]

Words

regulation n. 规定	cheat v. 欺骗；作弊
appointment n. 预约；约定	specific adj. 特定的
absent（from）adj. 缺席	excuse n. 借口
pass away 去世	religious adj. 宗教的

Sentence

If you have difficulty in class，please make an appointment with your teacher. 如果你听课有困难，可以约见老师寻求帮助。“have difficulty in doing”表示在某方面有困难；“make an appointment”意为“预约，约定”，后面跟 with 表示“与谁约定”，还可接 to do 表示“约定去干某事”，如 I’d like to make an appointment with my doctor. 我要和我的医生预约。

[文章大意]

美国的校规

每个学校都有校规，规定学生哪些事可做，哪些事不能做。不同的学校校规不同，但有些准则是一致的，比如美国很多学校都要求学生按时到校，独立完成作业，考试不能作弊等。当然，如果你听课有困难，可以约见老师寻求帮助，老师会很乐意帮助你。有的学校对请假还有具体的规定，要求学生任何原因缺席都需出示家长的请假条。可以允许的缺勤理由是个人生病、家人亡故或宗教节日。

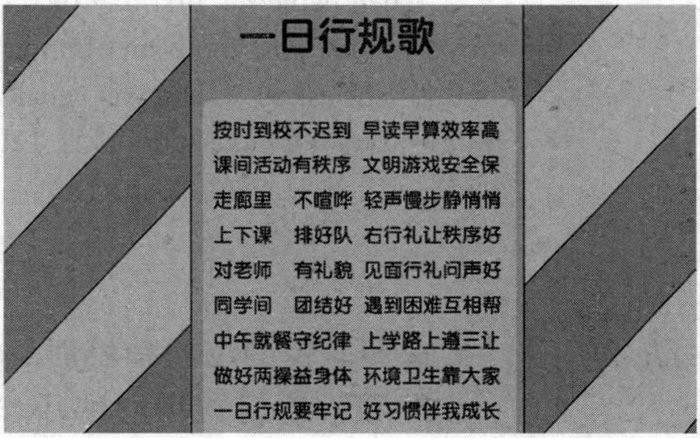

知识链接

校训（school motto）是指用比较醒目的词语来表达一个学校的校园文化和教育理念，是学校历史和文化的积淀。几个著名大学的校训分别为：

哈佛大学（Let Plato be your friend，and Aristotle，but more let your friend be truth. 与柏拉图为友，与亚里士多德为友，更要与真理为友）；

耶鲁大学（Light and truth 光明与真理）；

牛津大学（The Lord is my Light 主是我的亮光）；

剑桥大学（From here，light and sacred draughts 启蒙之所，智慧之源）；

北京大学（爱国，进步，民主，科学 Patriotism，Advancement，Democracy and Science）；

清华大学（自强不息，厚德载物 Self-discipline and Social Commitment）。

扩展阅读

Who Would Cry?

The six-year-old John was terribly spoiled（溺爱）. He would cry and throw away things when Mom doesn't give what he asks.

Then came his first day of school. When he came home from school，his mom met him at the door. "Was school all right?" she asked，"Did you get along all right? Did you cry?"

"Cry?" John asked. "No，I didn't cry，but the teacher did!"

动动手

1. 你们学校的校规和校训是什么？
2. 思考：还记得中国的小学生守则吗？和美国的学生守则有哪些不同？

第2章

Science

奥妙科学

What Causes the Color We See
颜色是怎么形成的

知识点 To know the knowledge about color
了解颜色的形成

What Causes the Color We See

Light is made up of colors. Where there is light，there is color. The color of any object depends on the color of the light rays reflected to our eyes. An apple looks red because it reflects the red rays of light. The sea looks blue because it reflects the blue rays. When there is no light，there is no color. A tree is green when we see in light，but it is black at night.

[**Notes 注释**]

Words

light n. 光　　object n. 物体　　reflect v. 反射　　ray n. 光线

depend on 依靠；取决于

Sentences

Light is made up of colors. 光线是由各种颜色组成的。"Be made up of" 意思是"由什么组成"，如 It is made up of time. 它是由时间组成的。

Where there is light，there is color. 哪里有光，哪里就有颜色。全句相当于：There is color in the place where there is light. 这是一个常用的句型，日常生活中可以灵活套用。如：Where there is a will，there is a way. 世事无难事，只要有心人。

[文章大意]

颜色是怎么形成的

光线是由各种颜色组成的。哪里有光，哪里就有颜色。物体的颜色取决于反射到我们眼中的光线的颜色。一个苹果看上去是红的，那是因为它反射出红色的光线。海洋看上去是蓝色的，是因为它反射出蓝色的光线。没有光也就没有颜色。一棵树，我们在光线下看是绿色的，而在夜里，它却变成了黑色。

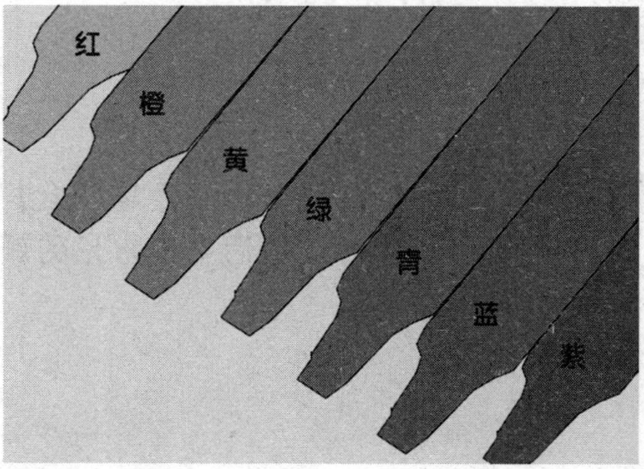

第2章 奥妙科学

知识链接

安全色是用以表达安全信息的颜色。用不同的颜色表示不同的安全度。国际标准化组织（ISO）和很多国家都对安全色的使用有严格规定。中国已制订了安全色国家标准，且规定用红、黄、蓝、绿四种颜色作为我国通用的安全色。

扩展阅读

The Pair of Shoes

A policeman comes to the office with one black shoe and one white shoe. His boss starts to yell at him，“Look at your shoes！ What colour are they? You are damaging police reputation. Go home and change the shoes.”

The policeman goes home at once，and comes back after a while.

“Boss，I have a problem. The other pair of shoes at home is black and white，too.”

动动手

1. 彩虹的七种颜色是什么？
2. 思考：生活中最常见的颜色是什么？

How Can We Divide the Seasons
季节的划分

知识点 To know how the seasons are divided
了解四季的划分根据

How Can We Divide the Seasons?

We all know there are four seasons in a year: spring, summer, autumn and winter. But how can we divide the seasons?

In the past, Chinese people thought Spring Commences (on the 4th of February) is the beginning of spring, Summer Commences (on the 6th of June) is the beginning of summer, Autumn Commences (on the 7th of August) is the beginning of autumn, and Winter Commences (on the 7th of November) is the beginning of winter. It is also said that spring is from March to May, summer is from June to August, autumn is from September to November, and winter is from December to February next year. There is still another way to define the season by average temperature in five successive days. When the average temperature is above 22 degrees, it is summer; when it is less than 10 degrees, it is winter. When it is between 10 to 22 degrees, it would be spring or autumn.

[**Notes 注释**]

Words

Spring Commences n. 立春　Summer Commences n. 立夏

Autumn Commences n. 立秋　Winter Commences n. 立冬

define v. 定义　average adj. 平均的　temperature n. 温度

successive adj. 连续的　degree n. 度　less than 小于、少于

Sentence

We all know there are four seasons in a year. 大家都知道一年有四个季节。“we all know”意思是大家都知道，也可根据情境不同翻译成“我们都知道、谁都知道”。相似词汇有：as we know 众所周知、正如我们所知；as we all known 众所周知、正如我们所知；as it is known to all 众所周知、正如我们所知。

[文章大意]

四季的划分

一年四季春夏秋冬是怎么划分的呢？

过去中国古人把立春（2 月 4 日）看成是春天的开始，立夏（5 月 6 日）是夏天的开始，立秋（8 月 7 日）是秋天的开始，立冬（11 月 7 日）是冬天的开始。也有人把 3~5 月定为春季，6~8 月为夏季，9~11 月为秋季，12 月到次年的 2 月为冬季。还有人根据连续 5 天平均气温来划分四季。连续 5 天平均气温在 22℃以上，就进入夏季；连续 5 天平均气温在 10℃以下，就进入冬季；连续 5 天平均气温在 10℃ ~ 22℃之间为春秋季。

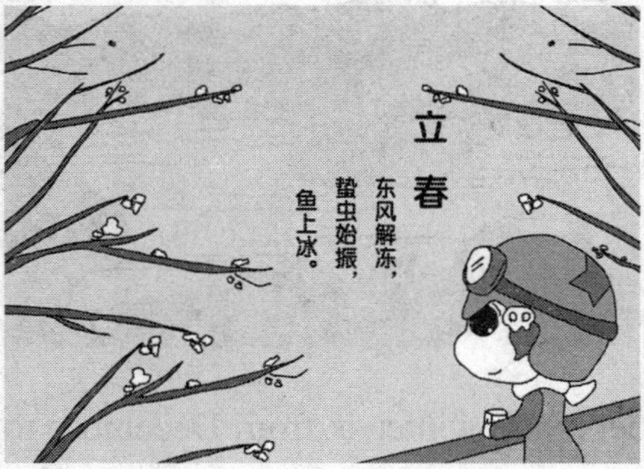

知识链接

南半球的季节与我们北半球的季节是相反的。当我们进入炎热的夏季时，他们则进入严寒的冬天。而我们历经严冬时，他们又阳光明媚了。

扩展阅读

Spring Is Coming

One day，there was a blind man sitting on the steps（楼梯）of a building with a sign by his feet，which read，"I am blind，please help."

A creative（有创造力的）young man was walking by the blind man and put a few of his own coins in the hat. He saw that the man only had a few coins in his hat. He wanted to help the poor blind man. Without asking for permission（同意），he took the sign，turned it around，and wrote a new message. He then placed the sign by the feet of the blind man and left.

Later that afternoon the creative young man returned by the blind man and noticed that his hat was almost full of bills and coins. The blind man recognized his footsteps and asked if it was he who had changed his sign. He also wanted to know what the man wrote on it. The young man said，"I just changed the words to make people know better."

The blind man can never see the sign— "Spring is coming，but I cannot see it."

动动手

1. 以"MY FAVOURITE SEASON"为题写一篇80字左右的作文。
2. 思考：你还能为这位盲人想出哪些口号让他得到更多的钱？

Meteor Shower
流星雨

知识点 To know what meteor shower is
了解什么是流星雨

Meteor Shower

In the universe, there are many dusts and blocks besides stars and planets. They have one name—meteoroids, and they also turn around the sun. But when the earth passes through them, the meteoroids may fall onto the earth because the Earth's gravity changes their ways. They fall very quickly and produce heat and light. Thus, people on the earth will see a bright light line in the sky which is what we call the meteor, or falling star. When many meteors fall to the earth, we call it meteor shower.

In order to record easily, people name different meteor shower after their different directions and positions. For example, each year on November 17th, a meteor shower at the Lions will occur, so it is named the Leonid meteor shower. There are also other popular meteor showers like Orion meteor shower, the Perseids meteor shower.

[**Notes 注释**]

Words

universe n. 宇宙　　star n. 恒星　　planet n. 行星

meteoroid n. 流星体　　earth's gravity 地球引力

meteor n. 流星　　meteor shower 流星雨

Sentences

In the universe，there are many dusts and blocks besides stars and planets. 在宇宙中，除了恒星和行星，还有许多尘埃和石块。"besides" 为介词，意思是"除……之外（还有）"，如 He has another car besides this one. 除了这辆车外，他还有一辆。

In order to record easily，people name different meteor shower after their different directions and positions. 为了方便记录，人们根据流星雨不同的方位给它们起了不同的名字。"name…after…" 意思是"以……命名"，如 The company is named after her name. 公司以她的名字命名。

[**文章大意**]

流星雨

在宇宙中，除了恒星和行星，还有许多尘埃和石块，它们叫做流星体，它们也绕着太阳转。但是，当地球从这些流星体中经过时，地球引力会改变流星体的运行轨道，导致它们掉落到地球上。他们掉落的速度非常快，并且会产生光和热。这样一来，地球上的人们就会看到天空中有一道明亮的光线闪过，那就是我们说的"流星"。当有很多流星落入地球时，我们就叫它流星雨。

为了方便记录，人们根据流星雨不同的方位给它们起了不同的名

字。例如每年 11 月 17 日前后出现的流星雨辐射点在狮子座中，就被命名为狮子座流星雨。其他有名的流星雨还有猎户座流星雨、英仙座流星雨。

知识链接

狮子座流星雨在每年的 11 月 14 至 21 日左右出现。一般来说，流星的数目大约为每小时 10 至 15 颗，但平均每 33 至 34 年狮子座流星雨会出现一次高峰期，流星数目可超过每小时数千颗。由于狮子座流星雨的中心点是狮子座，因而得名。

扩展阅读

Catch a Falling Star

Catch a falling star and put it in your pocket,
Never let it fade away;
Catch a falling star and put it in your pocket,
Save it for a rainy day.
For love may come and tap you on the shoulder
Some starless night,
And just in case you feel you wanna hold her,
You' ll have a pocketful of starlight

动动手

1. 去看看流星雨吧！
2. 思考：人们说对着流星许愿就一定能实现愿望，你这样做过吗？有用吗？

Why Do We Sweat
人为何出汗

知识点 To know why people sweat
了解人为什么出汗

Why Do We Sweat

The temperature of people's body is constant, and it is generally about 37℃. It is controlled by the temperature regulation center（体温调节中枢）in the nervous system, so that the body can make a balance between producing heat and releasing heat.

After eating some food, people can get energy. A part of this energy will be used for people's work or other activities, and another part of the energy will just release to the outside in form of heat. Through the releasing process, the body was able to keep a certain temperature. The skin is the main channel for releasing heat. When the outside temperature is higher than skin temperature（33℃）, sweating became the main way to release heat. In summer, the temperature is often above 30℃, and some times up to 38℃, sweating becomes the main or only way to release heat. Therefore, people sweat the most in summer.

[**Notes 注释**]

Words

temperature n. 温度；体温 constant adj. 恒定的

nervous system 神经系统 balance n. 平衡

release v. 排放 channel n. 渠道

Sentences

so that the body can make a balance between producing heat and releasing heat. 这样身体就能在产热和散热之间保持平衡。"To make a balance between A and B" 表示"在A和B之间保持平衡", balance做名词。Balance还可以做动词，表示相同意思时用balance between A and B。如：It's hard to keep a balance /balance between advising children and controlling them. 在给孩子提建议和控制他们之间很难找到合适的平衡点。

Therefore, people sweat the most in summer. 所以夏天人最爱出汗。"Therefore" 相当于so，但比so更正式。如The new boots are lighter and softer, and therefore more comfortable to wear. 新靴子更轻更软，因此穿起来也更舒服。

[**文章大意**]

人为什么会出汗

人的体温是恒定的，一般保持在37℃左右，由神经系统调节中枢控制，使身体产热和散热保持相对平衡。

人们吃进食物，就会获得能量，这些能量一部分供人们保持正常的工作活动，一部分以热的形式向外界发散。通过散热过程，身体才得以保持恒定的体温。皮肤是人体散热的主要渠道。当外界温度高于皮肤温度（33℃）时，出汗便成了人体主要的散热方式。夏天，气温经常在30℃以上，有时可高达38℃，出汗就成了人体主要或唯一的散热方式。因此，夏天人们出汗最多。

知识链接

汗腺和毛发、皮脂腺、指（趾）甲一样，都是皮肤的附属器。汗腺的主要功能是排泄汗液。大家都有汗流浃背的经验，所以很多人以为人体汗腺分布最多的地方是背部。其实，手掌和脚掌才是人体汗腺最多的地方，平均每平方厘米就有400条汗腺，而背部每平方厘米只有约80条汗腺。

扩展阅读

Girls Are Made Not Only of Water but Sweats

You can always smell a good scent（香味）from a girl. And boys feel very happy when a girl is passing them because they can smell this scent.

It was a hot summer day，beautiful girl was running towards the boy. When the girl was passing him，he took a deep breath and tried to keep the scent in his mind. However，the boy just kept silent then.

The boys next to him looked at him with contempt（鄙视）and said："What are you doing? Do you still taste the scent?"

The boy just touched his nose for a few times and said with disappointment："the fact is that girls are not only made of water but also sweats! It smells so terrible!"

动动手

1. 测一测你自己的体温。
2. 思考：汗水是从哪儿流出来的呢？

How Does Wind Form
风是怎么形成的

知识点 To know the formation and function of wind
了解风的形成和利用

How Does Wind Form?

Have you ever wondered how the wind is formed? In fact, the flowing of air forms the wind. Everywhere on the earth just absorbs the heat of the sun. However, they will absorb different amount of heat because of different locations. So the temperatures of the air may be different in different places, and the warm air will rise while the cold air will fall down. This kind of flowing of the warm air and cold air just makes a wind.

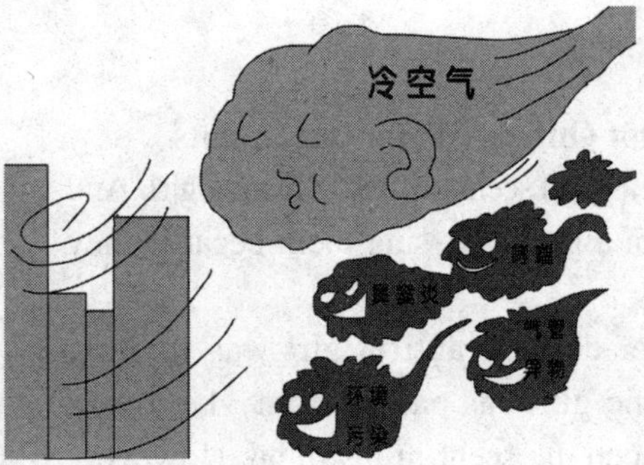

[**Notes 注释**]

Words

wonder v. 想知道　　absorb v. 吸收

amount of 大量的　　location n. 位置

Sentence

However, they will absorb different amount of heat because of different locations. 但是由于所处地点不同，不同地方吸收的热量不等。"because of" 意思是 "由于、因为"，和 because 的意思相同，但用法不同。because 后边要接一个完整的句子，而 because of 后边接名词或动名词。例如，"因为生病了，所以我没有去上学。" 这句话有两种翻译：I didn't go to school because of my illness. 或 I didn't go to school because I was ill.

[**文章大意**]

风是怎么形成的

你想过风是怎么形成的吗？简单来说，风是由于空气流动形成的。地球上任何地方都在吸收太阳的热量，但是由于地面每个部位受热不均匀，空气的冷暖程度就不一样。于是，暖空气会上升，冷空气会下降，这样冷暖空气便产生流动，形成了风。

知识链接

风能作为一种清洁的可再生环保能源，越来越受到世界各国的重视。但风速大于每秒 4 米才适宜于发电。据测定，一台 55 千瓦的风力发电机组，当风速为每秒 9.5 米时，机组的输出功率为 55 千瓦；当风速每秒 8 米时，功率为 38 千瓦；风速每秒 6 米时，只有 16 千瓦；而风速每秒 5 米时，仅为 9.5 千瓦。可见风力愈大，经济效益也愈大。

扩展阅读

How Does Rain Form?

In the high sky，the temperature is very low，so the vapor（水汽）there will become droplet（小水滴）. And these droplets will touch each other and then mix together with each other. It will get bigger and bigger. When it is so big that the air cannot hold it，it will fall down from the sky. When the temperature in low sky is above 0℃，the rain will be formed.

动动手

1. 为了测量风的大小，人们把风分为不同的等级，去了解一下风级是怎么划分的吧！
2. 思考：我们了解了风和雨的形成，那么闪电和雷是怎么形成的？

Where Does Salt Come from
盐是怎么来的

知识点 To know how salt is drilled
了解盐的开采方法

Where Does Salt Come from?

Most of the salt in our country comes from the sea. People dig pools and let seawater in. When the sun dries up the water, people can get salt from the ground. Salt is white, clean and beautiful.

There are a lot of salt wells in Sichuan Province of China. A salt well is much like a water well. People bring the well water up from under the ground and then dry it in big jars over fire. In this way they can get salt.

We can also get salt from salt mines. A salt mine may be found under the ground. Some years ago, people in Jiangxi Province found a big salt mine and soon opened it up. People there do not need salt from other places any more.

There are many salt lakes in the northwest of our country. Some of these lakes contain enough salt for our people to use for centuries.

[**Notes 注释**]

Words

dig v. 挖　　dry up（使）干涸　　salt well 盐井

salt mine 盐矿　　salt lake 盐湖　　open up 开发、打开

Sentence

People there do not need salt from other places any more. 那里的人不再需要其他地方的盐了。“not any more” 意思是 “不再”。要注意 not any longer 和 not any more 的用法区别：not any longer 表示动作或状态的 “不再”，not any more 表示次数的 “不再”。

[**文章大意**]

盐

在中国，我们用的盐大部分来源于海洋。人们挖好池塘，把海水引进来。太阳晒干池里的水分后，池底就是洁白、干净的盐了，非常漂亮。

四川还有大量盐井用于产盐。盐井和水井类似。人们把地下水通过盐井取出来，然后装进大罐子里用火烧。这种方法也能帮助人们得到盐。

盐矿也可产盐。几年前，人们在江西发现了一个大盐矿并开发出来，江西地区再也不需从其他地方进盐了。

中国西北还有盐湖。这些盐湖里的盐够我们用几百年。

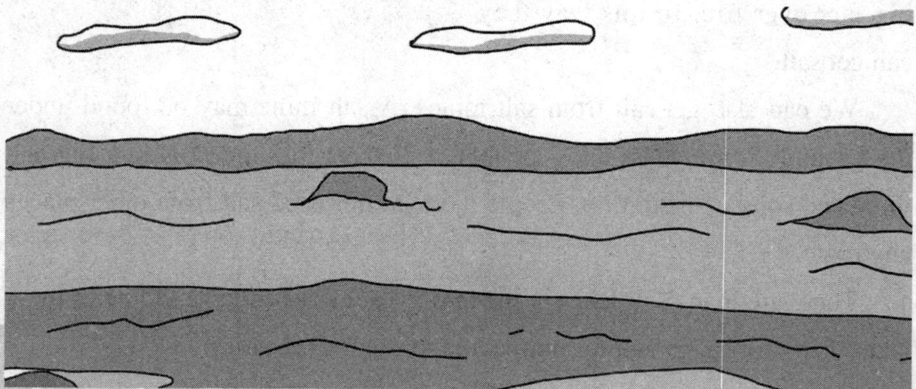

知识链接

除了提升食物的口味，食盐在日常生活中还有许多用途。蔬菜先放在盐水里泡一泡，可以去除虫子；喝咖啡时稍加一点盐，味道会更好。想要美白牙齿吗？用盐或是在牙膏里加点盐吧！

扩展阅读

Why Does Salty Food Make Us Thirsty（口渴的）

We need salt in our bodies to keep healthy. But the amount of salt in our body must be kept exactly right. It is said that we do not need to have more than 6 grams（克）of salt for one whole day. When the salt we have is more than what we need, the body rid itself of（去掉）the extra（额外的）salt by washing it away with water through kidney（肾脏）. If the food we eat is very salty, the body loses a lot of water in order to get rid of the extra salt, so we become thirsty.

动动手

1. 记一记。

   above the salt 坐上席

   old salt 经验丰富的老水手

   rub salt in a wound 在伤口上撒盐

   the salt of the earth 诚实优秀的普通人；社会中坚

   take sth. in a pinch of salt 半信半疑

   worth your salt 称职的；胜任的

2. 思考：人每天需要的盐是多少？如果摄入过量的盐有什么危害？

The Moon
月亮

知识点 To know the basic facts about moon
了解有关月亮的基本知识

Little Monkeys Catch the Moon

One day, a little monkey is playing beside a well. He looks into the well and shouts loudly: "Oh! My god! The moon has fallen into the well!" An old monkey runs over to take a look, and then he says, "Goodness! The moon is really in the water!" A group of monkeys run over to the well.

They look at the moon in the well and shout: "The moon does fall into the well! Come on! Let's get it out!"

Then, the old monkey hangs on the tree upside down, with his feet on the tree. And he pulls the next monkey's feet with his hands. All the other monkeys follow, and they join each other one by one down to the well. Just before they reach the moon, the old monkey raises his head and sees the moon in the sky. He yells excitedly: "Don't be so silly! The moon is still in the sky!"

[**Notes 注释**]

Words

shout v. 大喊　　run over to 跑过去　　take a look 看了一下

My god 我的天、天哪　　Goodness 天哪　　a group of 一群

Come on 快来　　each other 彼此、互相　　yell v. 大叫

silly adj. 傻的

Sentence

They look at the moon in the well and shout: "The moon does fall into the well! Come on! Let's get it out!" 他们看到井里的月亮，喊道："月亮掉在井里头啦！快来！让我们把它捞起来！" The moon does fall into the well 也可以表达为 The moon falls into the well，这里把 does 放在动词原形前面，是为了加强该动词的语气，例如：Do come to my birthday party. 一定来参加我的生日宴会。I do miss you. 我确实想你。

[文章大意]

猴子捞月

一天，有只小猴子在井边玩耍。它往井里一瞧，高喊道："噢！我的天！月亮掉到井里头啦！"一只大猴子跑来一看，说，"糟啦！月亮掉在井里啦！"一群猴子跑到井边来，他们看到井里的月亮，喊道："月亮掉在井里头啦！快来！让我们把它捞起来！"

然后，大猴子倒挂在大树上，拉住小猴子的脚，其他的猴子一个个跟着，它们一只连着一只直到井里。就在他们快要摸到月亮的时候，大猴子抬头发现月亮挂在天上呢！它兴奋地大叫："别蠢了！月亮还好好地挂在天上呢！"

知识链接

与月亮有关的英语词汇：
moon away 虚度时光
Don't moon away the Mid-autumn Festival.
找点事儿做吧，不要虚度了中秋佳节哦。
over the moon 欣喜若狂
She is over the moon about the two holidays.
连着两个节假日，她高兴极了。

扩展阅读

The Moon

The Moon is the only natural satellite of Earth, and it is closest to Earth than any other bodies in our solar system(太阳系). The distance between the Moon and the Earth is about 384401 kilometers. It's really a long distance!

The Moon is the second brightest thing in our sky, and the first is the Sun. But the Moon cannot shine itself. We can see the moon just because it reflects the light from the Sun. In the 1600s, Galileo, a famous Italian scientist, first observed the Moon through a telescope（望远镜）. He saw some dark spots and he thought that they were oceans.

Today, we know more about the Moon. We know that nothing lives on the Moon, and there are no oceans（海洋）, but only plains full of stones. Moon is the only place in space that human beings have visited so far.

动动手

1. 查查关于月亮的知识吧!
2. 思考：如果人类可以移民到月球，你愿意去吗？为什么？

第3章

Environment

积极环保

Tips for Environmental Protection
环保小点滴

知识点 To know what children can do to protect our environment 了解环保小点滴

Tips for environmental protection

Everyone is responsible for the environmental protection. We children should start from little things and work together to protect our homes. Usually we can do as follows：

1. Always remember to turn off the tap.

2. Reuse the water. For example，after we wash face or clothes，the water left can be used to wash floor or the bathroom.

3. Bring our own basket to buy food. When we are doing shopping with mom，we should not use plastic bags but use our own cloth bag or basket.

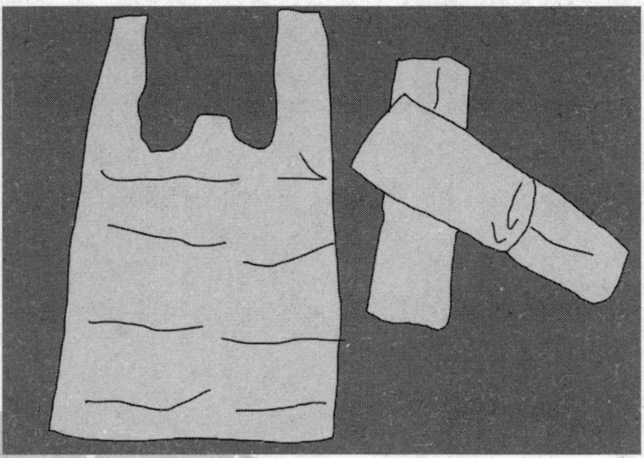

4. Never use disposable chopsticks.

5. Make full use of blank paper and recycled paper.

6. Never eat food made of wild animals.

7. Do not throw away used battery

casually.

As long as we start from these little things, the future sky must be blue, the water must be clear, and there will be a lot of flowers and trees around us. We can enjoy our nature.

[**Notes 注释**]

Words

responsible（for）adj. 负责的　　turn off 关（水 / 电）

tap n. 水龙头　　disposable chopsticks 一次性筷子

make full use of 充分利用　　plastic bags 塑料袋

Sentences

Always remember to turn off the tap. “turn off” 的意思是“关闭”，如 Please turn off the TV because mother is sleeping. 请把电视机关掉，妈妈正在睡觉呢。

As long as we start from these little things, the future sky must be blue, the water must be clear, and there will be a lot of flowers and trees around us. 只要我们从小事做起，一起保护环境，未来的天空一定是蔚蓝的，水是清澈的，绿树成荫，鲜花遍地。“as long as” 意思是“只要……就……”，如 As long as you study hard, you can pass the exam. 只要你努力学习，就一定能通过考试。

[**文章大意**]

环保小点滴

保护环境，人人有责。小朋友们更是应该从小事做起，携手保护我们的家园，平时应该做到以下几点：

1. 顺手关水龙头。

2. 一水多用。例如，洗脸、洗衣后的水可以留下来擦地，冲厕所等。

3. 自带菜篮买菜。陪妈妈一起买东西时少用塑胶购物袋，上街购物时带上布袋子或菜篮子。

4. 吃东西时少用一次性筷子。

5. 充分利用白纸，尽量使用再生纸。

6. 不要食用野生动物。

7. 废电池不要随意丢弃。

只要我们从小事做起，一起保护环境，未来的天空一定是蔚蓝的，水是清澈的，绿树成荫，鲜花遍地，人类可以尽情享受大自然赋予我们的幸福。

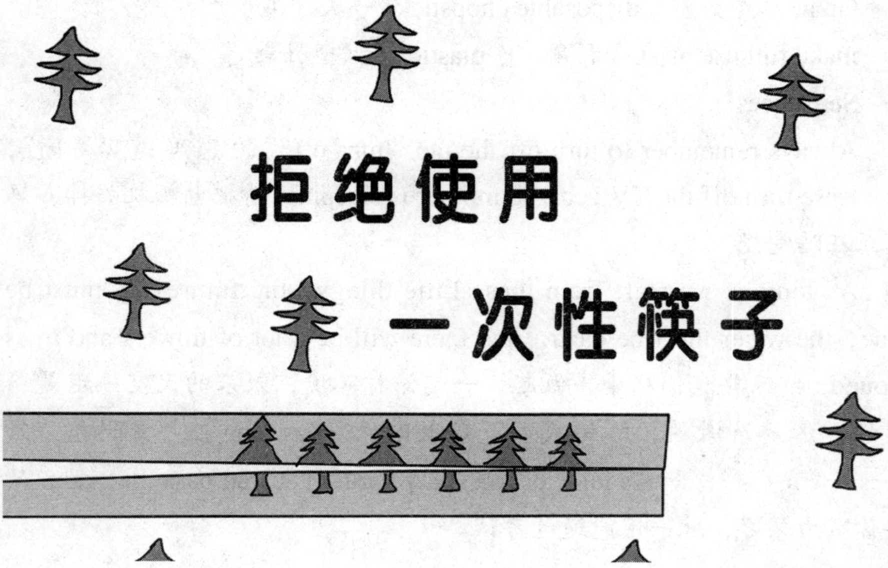

知识链接

每年6月5日是世界环境日（World Environment Day）。世界环境日的意义在于提醒全世界注意地球状况和人类活动对环境的危害。各国政府在这一天开展各种活动来强调保护环境的重要性。

扩展阅读

Do Not Forget to Wash Your Feet

One day, Tom's grandmother was ill, and his mom would go to another city to look after her. And she would stay there for a few days. Mom felt worried about Tom because he was a lazy boy. He would even go to bed without washing feet. So she said to Tom, "Tom, do not forget to wash your feet before you go to bed." Tom said, "Mom, why do we wash our feet every day?" Mom smiled, "You know if we do not wash our feet, it will smell (闻起来) bad. You are always so friendly to the environment!" Tom said, "No! If I do not wash my feet, it is friendly to the environment. Because it helps to save water."

动动手

1. 记住上面提到的环保小常识并在日常生活中实践。
2. 思考：环保与生活的关系是什么？

It Is Not Easy to Get Rid of Pollution
污染老大难

知识点 To know why it is not easy to get rid of pollution
了解为什么污染不容易彻底消除

It Is Not Easy to Get Rid of Pollution

Pollution is one of the most serious problems people are facing today. Everyone wants to get rid of pollution，but the pollution problem is still serious. Much pollution comes from the things that do good to people. For example，cars pollutes air while they are useful to people. Factories send out much material that pollutes air and water，but factories make necessary things for people. So in order to end pollution，people have to stop using many things，but many people do not want to do that. We must find ways to

stop pollution and at the same time not to have bad effect on our life.

［Notes 注释］

Words

pollution n. 污染 serious adj. 严重的

pollute v. 污染 factory n. 工厂

Sentence

We must find ways to stop pollution and at the same time not to have bad effect on our life. 我们必须找到一些方法，既不影响人们的正常生活，还能减少污染。“find ways to do” 意思是“找到做……的方法”，如 We should find ways to improve our study. 我们必须找到提高学习效率的方法。

［文章大意］

污染老大难

污染是现今人类面临的最为严重的问题之一。人人都想消除污染，但污染问题依然严峻。因为许多污染来自于对人类有益的事物，比如说，

汽车排放气体会污染空气，但汽车同时又对人类很有用；工厂会排放污染空气和水的物质，但工厂也会生产人类必需的物品。所以，要彻底消除污染，人类不得不停止使用很多习以为常的东西，这是很多人做不到的。我们必须找到一些方法，既不影响人们的正常生活，还能减少污染。

知识链接

细颗粒物（PM2.5）是对空气中直径小于或等于2.5微米的固体颗粒或液滴的总称。这些颗粒非常细小，肉眼是看不到的，它们可以在空气中飘浮数天。PM2.5主要对人体的呼吸系统和心血管系统造成伤害。PM2.5的浓度值以每立方米的微克值来表示，如10微克/立方米的PM2.5浓度指标为10。世界卫生组织（WHO）认为PM2.5指数小于10是安全值。

扩展阅读

Water Pollution

My grandfather often says that when he was young，the water in the river was clean. He often swam in the river with his friends. But now we cannot see such clean rivers. People threw rubbish into the river, and factories would discharged（排放）harmful chemicals（化学物品）into the river. The water in the river is getting dirtier. Many fish have died，and we cannot swim in the water. So we should protect the water from pollution.

动动手

1. 你还能想出其他方法来减少环境污染吗？
2. 思考：在你的生活中，你看到的最大的污染源是什么？应该怎样切断这些污染源呢？

Make Good Use of Waste Materials
废物利用

知识点 To know the ways of make use of waste material
了解废物利用的各种方法

Reuse Your Empty Glass Jars

If you have any empty glass jars，you could find some ways to reuse them!

1. Lantern（灯笼）—Paint the glass jar colorful. Put a candle in the glass jar，and light it for dining outdoors in the evening.

2. Flower vase— Glass jars make charming vases. You can paint them or tie a ribbon if you like. Then pick some flowers and put them in.

3. Snack jars— I like to keep nuts，raisins in glass jars. They stay fresh and convenient.

4. Bank— Jars make great banks. You could just cut a slot（小口）in the lid（盖子）to put change（零钱）in，and decorate the outside of the jar as you wish.

5. Candy jar— Decorate the jars as you likes. Fill it with candy or other favorite snacks and give it as a gift，or keep it on the table for guests to enjoy.

[**Notes 注释**]

Words

jar n. 广口瓶、罐子　reuse v. 再利用、重新使用　candle n. 蜡烛
snack n. 零食、小吃　raisin n. 葡萄干　decorate v. 装饰

Sentence

You could just cut a slot in the lid to put change in, and decorate the outside of the jar as you wish. 可以在盖子上剪开一个放零钱的小口，再随心装饰一下罐子就可以了。“cut a slot”表示“剪开一个小口子”；“as you wish”意为“随你所愿”，一般放在句子末尾，也可单独使用。

[**文章大意**]

空玻璃瓶的新生

如果你手上有空玻璃瓶的话，就来试试变废为宝吧！

1. 灯笼——用玻璃涂料把瓶子涂成彩色的。在玻璃瓶中放入一根蜡烛，点亮后就可以在户外享受烛光晚餐了。

2. 花瓶——玻璃瓶可以做成漂亮迷人的花瓶。你可以给瓶子涂上颜色，或系一条丝带装饰一番。然后去摘些花插进去。

3. 零食罐——我总是喜欢把坚果、葡萄干这些小零食装在玻璃罐里。这样既保证了食物的新鲜又很方便。

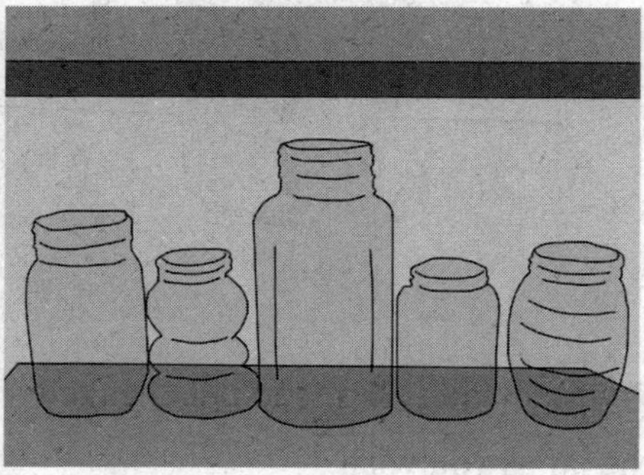

4. 储钱罐——玻璃罐是很好的储钱罐。可以在盖子上剪开一个放零钱的小口，再随心装饰一下罐子就可以了。

5. 糖果罐——可以随意装饰一番，装上糖果或是其他的零食，作为礼物送给朋友，或者放在茶几上供客人们品尝。

知识链接

环保词汇：
酸雨　acid rain
温室效应　greenhouse effect
森林覆盖率　forest coverage
绿化祖国　turn the country green
环保产品　environment-friendly products

扩展阅读

Earth Hour

Earth Hour started in 2007 in Sydney，Australia. At that time，2.2 million people and more than 2，000 companies turned their lights off（关灯）for one hour to oppose to（反对）the climate change. Only a year later，Earth Hour had become a world movement with more than 50 million people across 35 countries. It is held at 20：30—21：30 on the last Saturday of March.

Global landmarks（标志性建筑）such as the Sydney Harbour（海港）Bridge，Canada's National Tower in Toronto（多伦多），Golden Gate Bridge in San Francisco，and Rome's Colosseum（罗马圆形大剧场），all stood in darkness，as symbols of hope by the hour.

So do you have ever heard about this environmental activity? If yes，what do you think after the lights go back on? What else can you do to make a clean world？

动动手

1. 试试把空玻璃瓶利用起来吧。
2. 思考：你还知道哪些废物利用的方法？

The World Is Thirsty
地球口渴了

知识点 To know that water is limited and to save water
了解水资源的匮乏

The World Is Thirsty

The world is hungry, and it is also thirsty. This may seem strange to you, because nearly 70 percent（百分之）of the earth is covered with water. But about 97 percent of it is seawater. Man can only drink and use the other 3 percent fresh water from rivers, lakes and underground. And we cannot make full use of that, since some of it is in the form of iceberg. Even

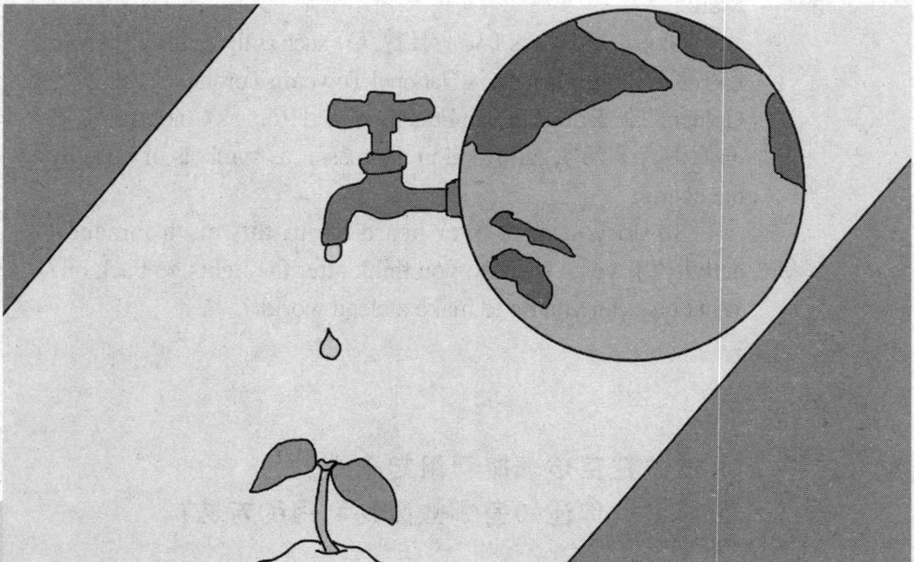

worse，some of it has been polluted. As we need more and more water，we must learn to save water.

［Notes 注释］

Words

thirsty adj. 口渴的 underground n./ adj. 地下 / 地下的 iceberg n. 冰山 be covered with 被覆盖

Sentence

This may seem strange to you，because nearly 70 percent（百分之）of the earth is covered with water. 可能你会觉得奇怪，因为地球表面百分之七十被水覆盖。"be covered with" 意思是"被……覆盖；……（上）铺着……"，如 The floor was covered with snow the next morning. 第二天一早，地面铺满了白雪。

［文章大意］

地球口渴了

地球很饿，也很渴。可能你会觉得奇怪，因为地球表面百分之七十被水覆盖，但97%的水是海水。人类只能利用剩下的3%——来自河

流、湖泊和地下的淡水。更糟的是，这些淡水还遭到了污染。所以随着用水量的增大，我们要学会节约用水。

知识链接

中国淡水资源总量为28，000亿立方米，占全球水资源的6%，仅次于巴西、俄罗斯和加拿大，居世界第4位，但人均只有2200立方米，仅为世界平均水平的1/4、美国的1/5，在世界上名列121位，是全球13个人均水资源最贫乏的国家之一。

扩展阅读

A Drop of Water

A drop of water is lying on the quiet and dark night. He looks at the sky and the pure moonlight. He feels very lonely.

Suddenly，there is a glare of lightning and a heavy rain falls from the sky. He quickly stands up and joins the rain all the way to a river. Here he sees a large number of brothers and sisters，so he feels very happy.

After that，he lives in the river with his brothers and sisters. They can greet the morning sun each day and say goodbye to sunset every day. He lives a happy life forever.

动动手

1. 读一读：

水，你是地球的血液。

Water，you are the blood of the earth.

没有你，地球上就没有生命。

Without you，we could not live.

水，你是地球的命脉，

Water，you are the life of the earth.

没有你，地球上就没有人类。

Without you，we could all die.

节约用水，人人有责。

Saving water is everyone's duty.

2. 思考：怎样避免出现“世界上最后一滴水是人类的眼泪”？

Refuse Sorting
垃圾分类

知识点 To know how to sort refuse
了解垃圾分类的基本常识

Refuse Sorting

Refuse is also called waste or rubbish. We often throw it away. But to protect our environment, we should separate the waste before throwing it away. Then how can we separate the waste?

There are usually four kinds of waste: recyclable rubbish, kitchen waste, harmful rubbish, and other waste. Recyclable rubbish can be reused. They are waste paper, plastic, glass, metal and cloth. All of these

should be put into the blue waste bins. The harmful rubbish includes waste battery，lamp，mercury，and outdated drugs. They are really harmful to the environment. So this kind of waste need special safe disposal.

[**Notes 注释**]

Words

refuse n. 垃圾（同义词有 waste 和 rubbish）　separate v. 分开

kitchen n. 厨房　recyclable adj. 可回收的　battery n. 电池

lamp n. 灯（管）　mercury n. 水银　outdated adj. 过时的

throw away 扔掉

Sentence

But to protect our environment，we should separate the waste before throwing it away. 但要保护我们的环境，我们必须在扔垃圾之前做好分类。本句中的“throw away”意思是“扔掉，丢弃”，如 I threw away all the broken toys. 我扔掉了所有的坏玩具。

[文章大意]

垃圾分类

对于垃圾（废物）我们通常是一扔了之。但要保护我们的环境，我

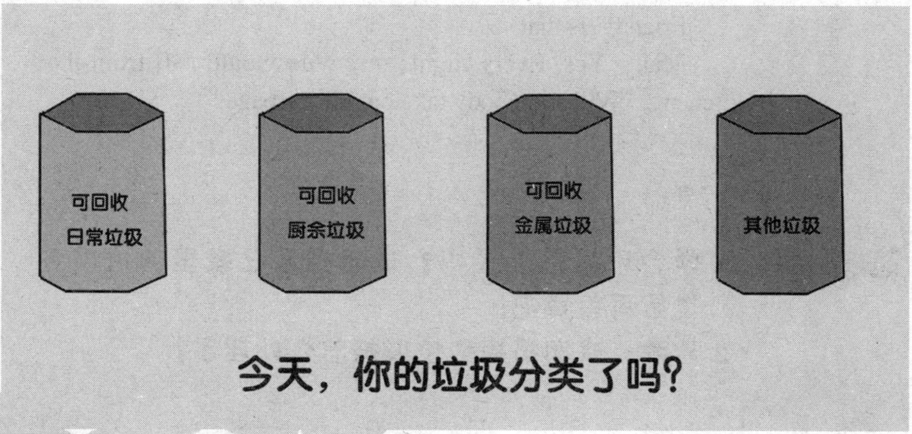

们必须在扔垃圾之前做好分类。垃圾是怎么分类的呢？

垃圾一般分为四类：可回收垃圾、厨余垃圾、有害垃圾，及其他垃圾。可回收垃圾是可以循环利用的，包括废纸、废旧塑料、玻璃、金属和布料。有害垃圾包括废电池、废日光灯管、废水银温度计、过期药品等，这些垃圾真的会对环境有害，需要特殊安全处理。

知识链接

就体积和重量而言，废电池在生活垃圾中是微不足道的，但它的害处却非常大。电池中含有汞、镉、铅等重金属物质。汞具有强烈的毒性，铅能造成神经紊乱、肾炎等；镉主要造成肾损伤以及骨骼疾病，如骨质疏松、软骨症及骨折。若把废电池混入生活垃圾中一起填埋，久而久之，渗出的重金属可能污染地下水和土壤，最终进入人类的食物链，给人类带来伤害。

扩展阅读

Will Somebody Take Out the Garbage

Man：In my house，I' m really somebody（双关语，表示“某人”或“重要人物”两个意思）.

Friend：Is that so?

Man：Yes. Every night，my wife would call from the kitchen，“Will somebody take out the garbage?”

动动手

1. 学会垃圾分类了吗？试着把自己家里的垃圾分类后再丢掉吧！
2. 思考：我们扔掉的垃圾被怎么处理了？

Wolong Natural Reserve

卧龙自然保护区

知识点 To know about the natural reserves in China
了解中国的自然保护区

Wolong Natural Reserve

Wolong Natural Reserve is the largest and most important natural reserve of giant panda in China. It is situated in Aba of Sichuan Province, about 130 kilometers away from Chengdu，the capital of Sichuan Province. The natural reserve was set up in 1963 to protect the national treasure of China—panda. In the area，there are many high mountains with all kinds of trees and flowers flourishing and with streams and rivers flowing around.So

it is important home to giant pandas. Now the natural reserve is famous all around the world. Foreigners would go there to see giant pandas.

[**Notes 注释**]

Words

natural reserve 自然保护区　situate v. 位于　capital n. 首都；省会

national treasure 国宝　flourish v.（长得）茂盛　stream n. 小溪

Sentence

In the area, there are many high mountains with all kinds of trees and flowers flourishing and with streams and rivers flowing around. 自然保护区里有许多高山，山上长满了各种花草树木，山间小溪小河缓缓流淌。句中“with all kinds of trees and flowers flourishing and with streams and rivers flowing around”是介词结构，修饰前面的名词 mountain，说明山上的具体情况。

[文章大意]

卧龙自然保护区

卧龙自然保护区是中国最大也是最重要的大熊猫保护区，位于四川

省阿坝州，距离省会成都130多公里。卧龙保护区建于1963年，是为专门保护中国国宝大熊猫而建的。保护区内高山林立，山上长满各种花草树木，山间小溪小河缓缓流淌，非常适宜大熊猫居住。如今，卧龙自然保护区享有世界声誉，外国朋友都喜欢到这儿来欣赏大熊猫。

知识链接

美国《生活科学》网站2008年评出全球十大最濒危的稀有动物物种，这些物种随时都有可能从这个地球上彻底消失。这十大濒危动物物种分别是苏门答腊犀牛、西部灰鲸、红狼、西伯利亚虎、黑脚貂、菲律宾鳄、山地大猩猩、恒河鲨、苏门答腊猩猩和加利福尼亚秃鹰。

扩展阅读

Lovely Pandas

Pandas' faces look like cats', but their fat bodies and short tails are like bears'. Pandas are very lovely and they are friendly to people. People like them very much. Most Pandas live in China. The northwestern part of Sichuan Province（省）and southern part of Gansu Province are their hometowns. Pandas like to climb trees. They usually live in the forests of high mountains, eat bamboo and drink spring water.

动动手

1. 你见过真正的大熊猫吗？到卧龙自然保护区去体验一下吧。
2. 思考：哪些原因可能造成动物濒临灭绝？

To Know Our Earth
了解地球

知识点 To know the seven continents and four oceans
了解七大洲和四大洋

Seven Continents and Four Oceans

Our earth looks like a water globe with only about 30 percent of land areas. We call them the Seven Continents . They are Asia, Africa, Europe, North America, South America, Antarctica and Oceania. They are considered to be one continent from the very beginning for they are connected or almost so. The water, covering about more than two thirds of the earth's surface, is made up of the four oceans. They are the Pacific, the Atlantic, the Indian and the Arctic Ocean. Asia is the largest continent,

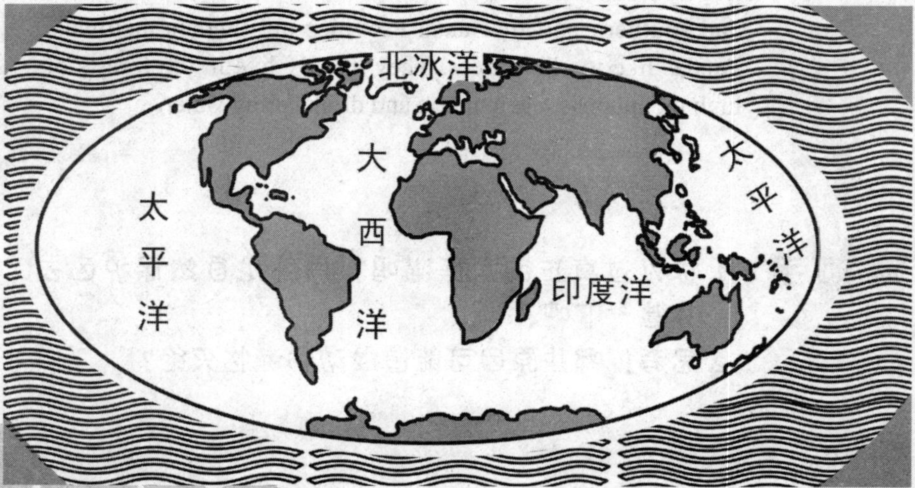

and Pacific is the largest ocean.

[**Notes 注释**]

Words

globe n. 球体；地球　　continent n. 大陆　　consider v. 认为

surface n. 表面　　ocean n. 海洋　　two thirds 三分之二

Sentence

The water, covering about more than two thirds of the earth's surface, is made up of the four oceans. 占地球表面三分之二的水构成了四大洋。"two thirds"意思是三分之二。英语中的分数由基数词构成分子，序数词构成分母；当分子大于一时，注意分母的序数词要用复数形式，如三分之一 one third；五分之三 three fifths。有的分数表达比较特殊，如二分之一 a half；四分之一 a quarter。

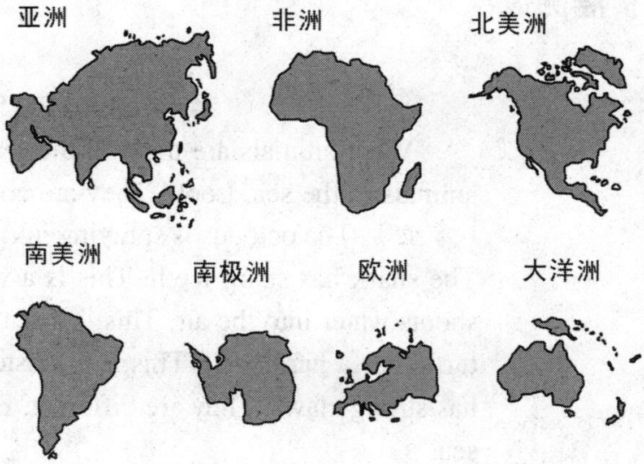

[文章大意]

七大洲和四大洋

咱们的地球其实更像个水球，表面只有大约 30% 的面积是陆地。这些陆地构成了七大洲，分别是亚洲、非洲、欧洲、北美洲、南美洲、南极洲和大洋洲。也有人认为这些陆地是一个大洲，因为最初这些陆地几乎是完全连接在一起的。另外约三分之二的面积全是水，形成了地球上的四大洋：太平洋、大西洋、印度洋和北冰洋。世界上最大的洲是亚洲，最大的洋是太平洋。

知识链接

太平洋南起南极地区，北到北极，西至亚洲和大洋洲，东接南、北美洲。约占地球面积的三分之一，是世界上最大的大洋，其面积是第二大洋大西洋面积的2倍。

扩展阅读

Animals in the Sea

What animals are there in the sea? There are all kinds of animals in the sea. Look! They are coming. This is an octopus（章鱼）. The octopus is spraying ink. This is a shark（鲨鱼）. The shark has sharp teeth. This is a whale（鲸）. The whale shoots water into the air. This is a sea turtle（海龟）. The sea turtle has a hard shell. This is a lobster（龙虾）. The lobster has strong claws. They are different. But all of them live in the sea.

动动手

1. 记一记各大洲和各大洋的英语名字。
2. 思考：海洋下面是什么？

第4章

Chinese Traditions

亲近传统

The Art of Calligraphy
书法艺术

知识点 To know the art of Calligraphy
了解中国的书法艺术

The Art of Calligraphy

Calligraphy (书法), also named Shu Fa, is a kind of Chinese traditional art. There are four basic skills for the ancient Chinese scholar (文 人): Qin (musical instrument), Qi (board game), Shu (calligraphy), Hua (painting). No one knows when Chinese characters came into the world. In Qin Dynasty (朝 代), Xiao Zhuan became the official (官 方 的) characters. At that time, calligraphy had been an art.

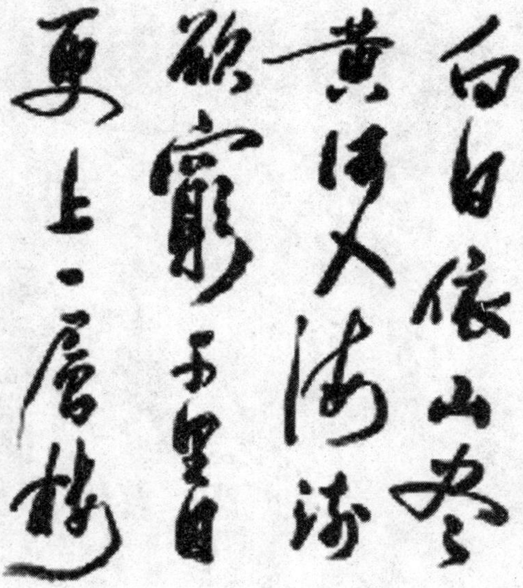

Chinese calligraphy is an oriental art. Like chopsticks, calligraphy was once entirely

Chinese, but as Chinese culture spread to Korea, Japan, and Singapore, calligraphy became a special feature of the oriental art.

[**Notes 注释**]

Words

ancient adj. 古代的　　feature n. 特征

character n. 字母 / 数字 / 符号（汉字通常用 Chinese character 或单独用 character 表示）　　oriental adj. 东方的（相当于 eastern，但更为正式）

Sentence

Like chopsticks, calligraphy was once entirely Chinese, but as Chinese culture spread to Korea, Japan, and Singapore, calligraphy became a special feature of the Oriental art. 像筷子一样，书法最初也完全是中国特有的，但是随着中国文化的普及，书法也流传到韩国、日本以及新加坡，成为东方艺术的奇葩。此句中第一个 Chinese 用做形容词，表示“中国特有的”，也可表达口语中的“很中国”，如 This dress is Chinese. 这件衣服很中国 / 这件衣服很有中国味道。

[**文章大意**]

书法

书法是一门中国艺术，是中国古代文人必须掌握的四种基本才能

（琴棋书画）之一。书法的准确诞生时间无人可知。但至少从秦朝起，人们就开始使用小篆作为官方文字。也是从那时起，书法成为一门艺术。

中国书法是东方艺术的一种，开始只是在中国普及，后来流传到韩国、日本以及新加坡，成为东方艺术的奇葩。

知识链接

书写汉字需要笔、墨、纸、砚四样东西，俗称“文房四宝”。其中最有名的上乘品是：湖笔、徽墨、宣纸、端砚。

扩展阅读

Wang Xizhi and *Lantingxu*

China has a large number of great calligraphers（书 法 家）, and the most famous one is Wang Xizhi. The most famous example of his writing is the *Lantingxu*（Preface to the Poems Composed at the Orchid Pavilion）, which recorded a famous gathering of some literary figures writing poems and enjoying the companionship of wine during the Tomb-sweeping Day（清 明 节）of 353AD. Wang’s work was written in the Xingshu, or “running script”, and has become the model for that particular style of writing.

动动手

1. 记一记：正确书法姿势：手要保持平直；将背挺直，确保眼睛和纸之间有一定的距离；双腿间保持一定距离。
2. 思考：王羲之是怎样成为书法家的？

Chinese Traditional Clothes
中国传统服饰

知识点 To know the colorful Chinese Traditional Clothes
了解绚丽多彩的中国传统服饰

The Cheongsam

The cheongsam or Qipao, comes from a kind of ancient clothing of Man nationality. In the past, people of Manchu wore long gowns. During the Qing Dynasty, cheongsam began to spread in the Central Plains of China. After the rule of the Qing Dynasty was overthrew by 1911 Revolution, this kind of traditional dress was saved and improved for Chinese woman. It became narrow-sleeved and fitted to the waist. Its hem extended to the ankles.

In this way，cheongsam became the uniform for woman；even students dressed themselves with it. Moreover，many foreign women like it very much. Today，there are many colorful cheongsams with different types.

［Notes 注释］

Words

be overthrew 被推翻　　1911 Revolution 辛亥革命

improve v. 改善；提高　　waist n. 腰　　ankle n. 脚踝

Sentence

In this way，cheongsam became the uniform for woman；even students dressed themselves with it. 就这样，旗袍成为中国女性的标准服装，甚至连学生也穿着旗袍。"in this way"或"in…way"表示"用……方式"，可用于句中或句首，如：He did this in the same way. 他用同样的方式完成。

［文章大意］

旗袍

旗袍来自于满族古老的服装，清朝时开始在中原流行起来。辛亥革命后清朝被推翻，但这种传统服饰却保存了下来，并被改良成了中国女性的标准服饰。女性旗袍由原来的宽袖改成窄袖，直筒裙变成紧身贴腰裙，裙边下摆延伸到脚踝处。

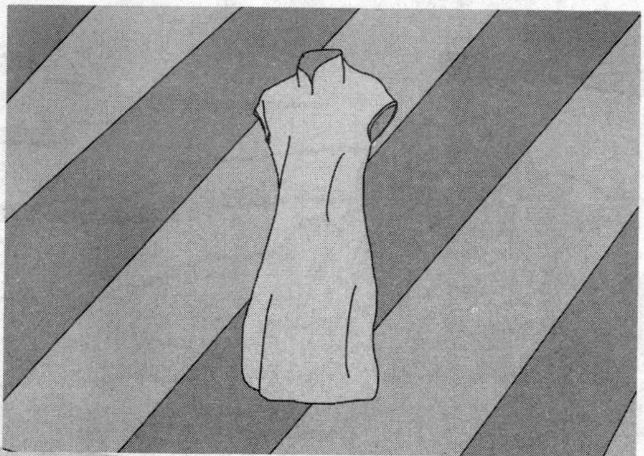

从此，旗袍成为中国女性的标准服装，甚至连学生也穿着旗袍。许多外国女性也很喜欢它。今天，我们可以看到许多色彩艳丽、各式各样的旗袍款式。

知识链接

中国现有56个民族，汉族人口最多，所以其他的民族就被称为少数民族。历史上有两个少数民族统一过中国，建立起了封建政权，分别是蒙古族建立了元朝（1271—1368），满族建立了清朝（1644—1911）。

扩展阅读

Chinese Traditional Clothes

China is a multi-national country. Each nation has traditional clothing of its own. Chinese clothing is very beautiful and colorful. It changes by area and time.We have Han Costumes，Tang Costumes and Cheongsam. The clothing materials are good and soft.

It also influences the clothing of neighboring countries. We can find，for example，something of Chinese Traditional Clothing in Japanese kimono（和服）and Korean Hanbok（韩服）.

动动手

1. MATCH THE ENGLISH AND CHINESE.

Cheongsam	韩服
Tang costumes	和服
Han Costumes	旗袍
kimono	汉服
Hanbok	唐装

2. 思考：你认为哪种服装最能代表中国？为什么？

Chopsticks
筷子

知识点 To know knowledge of Chopsticks 筷子

The Beginning of Chopsticks

Chopsticks are a pair of sticks with the same length. Chinese people use them to eat food. Not only used in China，they are also widely used in Japan，Korea and Vietnam（越南）and so on. When did the Chinese begin to use chopsticks? Nobody knows! It is said that in the ancient China，people cooked their food in a large pot，and somebody who hurried to eat food would break twigs off trees to get the food in the hot pots.

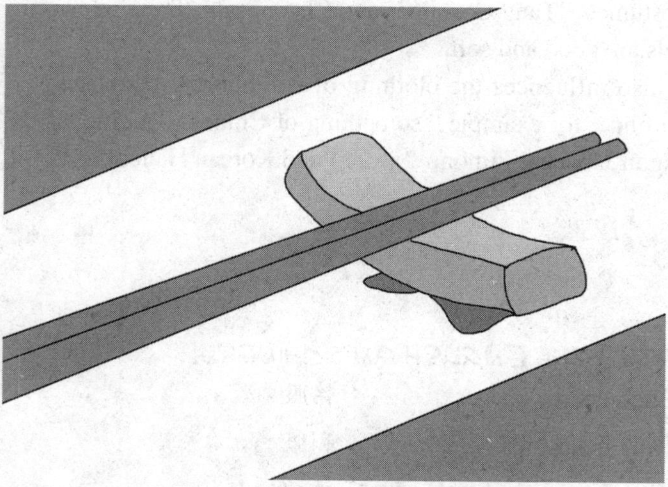

From then on，our ancestors have invented the first Chinese tableware. Because of this，most of chopsticks are made of bamboo and wood. Today，more and more foreign friends can use chopsticks as well as Chinese people.

[**Notes 注释**]

Words

stick n. 棍子　　twig n. 树枝（“树干”用 branch）　　bamboo n. 竹子

break off 折断　　ancestor n. 祖先　　tableware n. 餐具

Sentences

Chopsticks are a pair of sticks with the same length. 筷子是两只一样长度的细棍。“with the same length”在句子中补充说明 stick 的特征，所以称为补语。

…and somebody who hurried to eat food would break twigs off trees to get the food in the hot pots. 有些想急着早点吃到食物的人就折断树枝把食物从热锅里夹出来。“hurry”在句中做动词，表示“急匆匆地去干某事”，通常与 to 搭配，如 The telephone suddenly rang and she hurried to answer it. 电话突然想起来，她赶紧去接。Hurry 还可做名词，如 in a hurry（急忙）、in no hurry（不忙）等。

[文章大意]

筷子的来源

筷子就是两只一样长的细棍子，中国人用它来吃饭。并且，不仅中国人在用，日本、韩国和越南等地的人也使用筷子。中国人什么时候开始使用筷子呢？没有人知道答案！据说在古时候，中国人都是用大锅煮熟食物的，有些性子急的人想早点吃到嘴，就折断了树枝把滚烫的食物从锅里夹出来。

从那时起，我们的

祖先就发明了中国的第一种餐具。也正因如此，许多筷子都是用竹子和木头制作的。现在，越来越多的外国朋友也会用筷子了，而且用得和中国人一样好。

知识链接

古时候，人们有用骨头和玉石来制作筷子，在春秋时代又出现了铜制和铁制的筷子。富人家则用玉筷子或金筷子以显示其家庭的富有。许多帝王用银制的筷子以检查他们的食物中是否被人投了毒。

扩展阅读

Disposable Chopsticks（一次性筷子）

Disposable chopsticks were not invented by Chinese. The Japanese invented them and brought to China. Though they give us a lot of benefits，they do much harm to our earth. First，they waste the woods in the forests，and the trees may reduce；second，they may also produce a "greenhouse effect"（温 室 效 应），and the carbon dioxide（二 氧 化 碳）may increase.

动动手

1. 猜谜语：

They have long body. 身体细长，
They are two brothers. 兄弟成双，
They can only eat dishes. 只会吃菜，
But cannot drink soup. 不会喝汤。

2. 思考：你觉得用什么样的餐具更环保？

Chinese Surnames
中国百家姓

知识点 To know the knowledge about Chinese surnames
了解中国人姓氏相关知识

Chinese Surnames

Chinese surnames are passed down from generations and show the family history. Chinese people usually ask other people's surnames for the first meeting. If they have the same surname, they will feel happier because they think they come from the same family.

The book *A Collection of Chinese Surnames* listed 408 single-character surnames and 30 double-character ones. The largest populations in Chinese surnames are Li, Wang, Zhou, Zhang, Zhu and so on. Now, more and more Chinese focus on their family trees and family records.

[**Notes 注释**]

Words

surname n. 姓氏　　*A Collection of Chinese Surnames* 百家姓

single-character surname 单姓　　double-character surname 复姓

focus（on）v. 关注

Sentence

Now，more and more Chinese focus on their family trees and family records. 如今，越来越多的中国人开始关注自己的家谱和家史。“focus on”为英语中的搭配，意思是“关注；专注”，如 A student should focus on study but not games. 学生应专注于学习，而非游戏。

[文章大意]

中国姓氏

中国姓氏是一代一代传下来的，展示了家庭的历史。中国人初次见面时往往会询问别人的姓氏，如果碰巧同姓，他们就会开心，因为他们来自同一个家族。

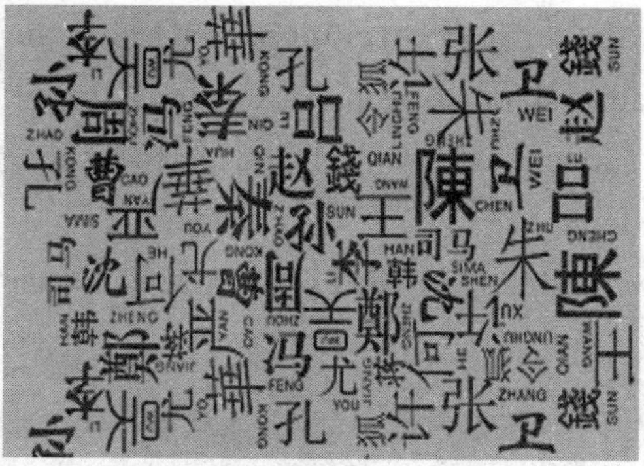

《百家姓》一书收录了 408 个单姓和 30 个复姓。其中最大的姓氏有李、王、周、张、朱等等。如今，随着中华传统文化越来越受关注，越来越多的中国人开始关注自己的家谱和家史。

知识链接

中国的姓氏有以下几种起源：第一，从地名、国名而来的姓氏，比如“赵”、“郑”和“苏”；第二，流传下来的古姓，如“任”和“漆”；第三，从祖先的名字中来的姓氏，有“高”、“黄埔”；第四，古代官职也可用为姓氏，比如“史”（史官）、“司徒”（管理土地的官员）。

扩展阅读

Chinese Names and Western Names

Chinese people and western people have different ways to name a person. The westerners put name（so they also call it first name）before surname. Take the name John Wilson for example. Wilson is the surname，and John is the first name；While Chinese people put name after surname，for example，in the name of Li Jun，Li is the surname and Jun is the first name. What causes this difference?

Chinese people think blood line is very important. Everyone is only one part of the whole family. So the surname，which stands for the family，is put before the name. The westerners think everyone as independent person，and the first name，which tells who you are，is put at the beginning.

动动手

1.背一背

The latest list of Chinese surnames

Zhang Wang Li Liu Chen Yang Huang Sun Zhou Wu

Xu Zhao Zhu Ma Hu Guo Lin He Gao Liang

2011 年中国最新姓氏排名

张王李刘陈杨黄孙周吴

徐赵朱马胡郭林何高梁

2.思考：你的姓是什么？它的历史是怎样的？

Tea
茶

知识点 To know the knowledge about tea
了解茶的相关知识

How Did Chinese First Drink Tea?

Chinese people drink tea every day, and the history of tea is full of colorful legends. It was said that Shen Nong, an emperor of ancient China, first discovered tea as a drink. As the legend goes, long time ago, people all drank water in the river or lake directly, so many people was ill. So Shen Nong asked that water should be boiled before drinking for health reasons. One day, when people were boiling water under a bush, some leaves fell into the water, turning the color of water into brown and having a pleasant odor. Shen Nong saw and drank this kind of brown water, then enjoyed the taste.

Afterwards, a man named Lu Yu invented a large number of cultivation and making methods of tea, which later were introduced to Japan, Portuguese, France and so forth. Tea becomes popular worldwide.

[**Notes 注释**]

Words

be full of 充满　as the legend goes 传说　long time ago 很久以前

fall into v. 落入　pleasant adj. 令人愉快的，舒适的　odor n. 气味

afterwards adv. 后来、然后　cultivation n. 培养、耕作

Sentence

Afterwards, a man named Lu Yu invented a large number of cultivation and making methods of tea, which later were introduced to Japan, Portuguese, France and so forth. 后来，一个叫陆羽的人发明了很多种植和配制茶叶的方法，这些配方后来也传到了日本、葡萄牙、法国等地。"afterwards" 意思是"后来"，同义词有 then，next，since，subsequently，都表示后来的意思。"a large number of" 表示"大量的、许多"，同义词有 many，much，a lot of，numerous，a large amount of 等。and so forth 意思是"等等"，同义词是 and so on，etc.

[**文章大意**]

中国饮茶的来源

中国人每天都会喝茶，茶的历史也是充满了多彩的传说。据说中国古代的神农大帝为了让百姓喝上干净卫生的水，要求大家必须把水煮沸后才能饮用。有一次，人们在一个灌木丛边烧水，树上的叶子掉进了正在烧的水里，水立即变成了褐色，还散发出一股木叶清香。神农见后，试着尝了一下味道，顿觉清爽不已，立即爱上了这个味道。

后来，一个叫陆羽的人发明了很多种植和配制茶叶的方法，这些配方后来也传到了日本、葡萄牙、法国等地，中国茶从此闻名世界。

知识链接

不同的地域种出的茶叶也有所不同。中国茶可分为五大类：绿茶、红茶、乌龙茶、紧压茶和花茶。最有名的茶叶有江苏的碧螺春、浙江的龙井、福建的铁观音以及云南的普洱茶等等。

扩展阅读

High Tea

Coming from the United Kingdom，high tea is a kind of afternoon tea. It was typically eaten between 3pm and 5pm. Because it was eaten at a high dining table rather than a low tea table，people call it high tea.

Different from Chinese tea，the high tea was added with both milk and sugar. Moreover，it would be drunk with a lot of sandwiches，scones（烤饼）and cakes. The food would be often served in a tiered stand.

动动手

1. 读一读这首小诗。

I’m a little Teapot.
I’m a little Teapot
Short and stout.
Here is my handle.
And here is my spout.
When the water’s boiling.
Hear me shout.
Lift me and pour me out.

2. 思考：茶和咖啡体现了哪些不同的文化？

The Chinese Zodiac
十二生肖

知识点 The Chinese Zodiac 十二生肖

Legend of Chinese Zodiac

One day, the twelve animals quarreled over who would be the head of them, so the god decided to hold a game: whoever reached the top of the mountain first would be the leader. All the animals get together to climb the mountain. When they were closing to the destination (终点), the rat jumped off the ox's back and won the game, and then the ox was the second. The lazy pig reached last. Therefore, the rat becomes the first animal in the cycle of Chinese zodiac; the ox is second; and the pig, last.

[**Notes 注释**]

Words

legend n. 传说　　quarrel (over) v. 争吵　　destination n. 终点

Sentence

One day, the twelve animals quarreled over who would be the head of them，so the god decided to hold a game：whoever reached the top of the mountain first would be the leader. 一天，十二个动物对于谁才是头儿争吵不休。于是，玉皇决定举行一个比赛：谁最先到达山顶就封谁为头儿。“quarrel” 意思是 “争吵，争论”，后面通常接介词 over 或 about；如果表示 “与谁争吵”，就需用介词 with。如：I hate quarrelling with you. 我不愿和你争吵。

[文章大意]

十二生肖

一天，十二个动物对于谁才是头儿争吵不休。玉皇决定举行一个比赛：谁最先到达山顶就封谁为头儿。于是所有的动物集合起来一起爬山。快要到达目的地时，老鼠跳过牛背抢先一步登上山顶，赢得了比赛；懒散的猪最后一个到达。十二生肖的顺序也就这样形成了：鼠第一，牛第二，猪最后。

知识链接

十二生肖和中国传统农历关系紧密。在夏商时期，聪明的中国先民就开始使用生肖了。到南北朝时，人们用一种动物代表一年，这一年出生的人就是这个生肖。渐渐地，形成了子鼠、丑牛、寅虎、卯兔、辰龙、巳蛇、午马、未羊、申猴、酉鸡、戌狗、亥猪的顺序。

扩展阅读

Tiger and Monkey

There are many animals living in the forest，like tiger，rabbit，monkey，squirrel and deer，etc. The king of this forest is tiger，who does not want to look for food，but asks other animals to bring him something to eat. One day he sees a monkey who is the cleverest animal in Chinese Zodiac and says，”I’m hungry，monkey. Go and bring me a fat pig.” “Oh，Tiger，” says the monkey. “I can’t do that now. There is another tiger over there. He also wants a fat pig. He will not let me get anything for you to eat. I am afraid of him.” “What?” cries the tiger，“Show me that tiger. I will teach him a lesson.” “Come with me！” says the monkey.

The monkey and the tiger get to a bridge over the river. “Now look down at the water，” says the monkey. “Do you see the head，the white teeth and the big green eyes of a tiger?” “Yes，I do，” says the old tiger，“I will eat him up!” “So you told Monkey not to bring me anything?! I’ll kill you!” With these words the tiger jumped into the river. He did not come out again. “Ha，ha，ha! Goodbye，Mr. Tiger.” said the monkey and he went away.

动动手

1. 连一连：

鼠	Rabbit	牛	Sheep
虎	Dog	兔	Tiger
蛇	Monkey	马	Cock
羊	Pig	龙	Rat
猴	Ox	鸡	Snake
狗	Dragon	猪	Horse

2. 思考：据说猫和老鼠是天敌也和生肖有关，你知道吗？

The Story of Nian
年的故事

知识点 To know the importance of the Spring Festival to Chinese 了解春节对中国人的意义

The Story of Nian

As the old legend goes, there was a monster named Nian. On every New Year's Eve —the 30th day of the last lunar month, the monster Nian would get out of the sea, eating villagers and destroying their fields and buildings.

Once on a New Year's Eve, Nian ran into a small village, killing almost all the villagers. Only two families were alive. The first family is a newly married (刚结婚) couple. They were safe because of wearing red wedding clothes, which looked like fire in Nian's eyes. And Nian was afraid of the fire, so it ran away. The other family was safe because their children were setting off firecrackers at that time. The loud noise scared Nian away.

Hence, people began to wear red clothes and set off firecrackers on New Year' Eve to keep the fierce monster Nian away.

[**Notes 注释**]

Words

monster n. 怪兽、怪物　lunar month n. 农历月　villager n. 村民

destroy v. 破坏　building n. 房子、建筑物　fierce adj. 凶猛的

wedding clothes n. 婚礼服装　firecracker n. 鞭炮　scare v. 惊吓

Sentence

And Nian was afraid of the fire，so it ran away. 害怕火的“年”跑开了。"Be afraid of sth.“是害怕某物的意思，那么“害怕做……”应该如何表达呢？有两种表达：be afraid of doing sth. 和 be afraid to do sth. 两者都表示“害怕做某事”的意思。但也有区别，be afraid to do sth. 的意思是“害怕做某事”，也就是对做某事内心感到恐惧；be afraid of doing sth. 表示内心里不情愿做某事，也可以说是不希望发生某事，但自己不一定能避免它。例如：He is afraid to touch the snake. 他不敢碰那条蛇。（他内心恐惧蛇。）He is afraid of eating onion. 他怕吃洋葱。（不是他敢不敢吃的问题，而他是不愿意吃。）“Run away”意思是逃跑、跑开。

[**文章大意**]

年

传说在很久以前，有一个叫“年”的怪兽。每到除夕日——农历十二月的最后一天，它就会从海里跑出来吃掉村民，还会毁坏田地和房屋。

又一个除夕夜，“年”冲进了一个小村庄，几乎吃掉了所有的人，只有两户人家幸存了下来。第一个家庭是一对新婚夫妇，当“年”冲进来时他们正穿着红色的婚服，“年”以为那火红的衣服是火，害怕火的它跑开了。另一户人家则是因为他们的孩子在家门口放鞭炮，巨响声吓走了“年”。

自此，人们就开始在除夕夜穿上红色的衣服，放鞭炮来吓走“年”这个凶猛的怪兽。

知识链接

农历又叫阴历，是中国流传久远的一种历法。每年12个月，大月30天，小月29天，全年354天或355天（一年中哪月大哪月小，年年不同）。由于平均每年的天数比公历年（太阳年）约差11天，所以在19年里设置7个闰月，有闰月的年份全年383天或384天。中国的很多节日都是根据农历来确定时间的。

扩展阅读

The Spring Festival Celebration

The Chinese Spring Festival Celebration usually lasts for 15 days. Celebratory（庆 祝）activities include Chinese New Year Feast，pasting up Spring Festival couplets（贴 春 联），setting off firecrackers，giving lucky money to children，the New Year bell ringing and Chinese New Year Greetings. Most Chinese people will stop the celebrating in their home on the 7th day of the Spring Festival because the national holiday usually ends around that day，however celebrations in public areas can last until the 15th day of New Year.

动动手

1. 记住这些祝福语。

龙年吉祥！ Good Luck in the Year of the Dragon!

恭喜发财！ May you come into a good fortune!

恭贺新年！ A happy New Year to you！

2. 思考：人们都说年味是一年不如一年了，你认为呢？为什么会有这种现象？

第5章

Foreign Cultures

放眼国际

April Fool's Day
愚人节

知识点 To know the beginning of April Fool's Day
了解愚人节的来历

The Beginning of April Fool's Day

In 1564, Charles IX, the French king, adopted the Gregorian calendar and fixed January 1st as New Year's Day. Those who were against the change continued to express their complaints by giving presents or paying New Year's visits on April 1st.In the following years, these traditionalists who insisted on celebrating the New Year at its old time were mocked as fools and people would play jokes on them and called them "Poisson d'avril"（法语）, meaning April Fish.

This must have been so much fun that it spread all over the world and people played tricks on everyone, not just the people who didn't accept the new calendar.

[**Notes 注释**]

Words

adopt v. 采用　　continue v. 继续　　celebrate v. 庆祝　　lunar 农历

calendar n. 日历　　Gregorian 格里高利历法，又称公历

insist on（doing）坚持　　play joke on=play trick on 开玩笑

Sentences

Those who were against the revision（改变）continued to express their complaints（抱　怨）by giving presents or paying New Year's visits on April 1st. 而那些反对这一改变的人则仍旧在4月1日送礼或进行新年旅行来表达他们的不满。"Be against" 意思是"反对"，如 He is against the plan. To pay a visit（to）拜访 / 访问（某人 / 某地）。

…these traditionalists who insisted on celebrating the New Year at its old time were mocked（嘲笑）as fools…那些依然遵循旧历庆祝新年的顽固派被当成了愚人……"traditionalist"一词来自于 tradition（传统）+al（传统的）+ist（传统的人 / 传统主义者）。"Mock"意为"嘲笑，戏弄"，嘲笑某人可用"mock（at）sb."或"make a mock of sb. Mock sb as…"嘲笑某人是……

[**文章大意**]

愚人节的起源

1564年，法国皇帝查尔斯九世正式采用格里高利历法（公历），规定每年的1月1日为新年。而那些不接受这一规定的人则仍旧在4月1日送礼或进行新年旅行来表示他们的不满。几年后，那些依然遵循旧历庆祝新年的顽固派被当成了愚人，其他人

会嘲笑和捉弄这些愚人，并戏称他们为“四月的鱼”，就是“愚人”的意思。

这一定是一件非常有趣的事，因为这个节日现在已经传遍世界各地，这一天人们不只捉弄那些顽固派，而是捉弄所有人。

知识链接

愚人节时，人们常常组织家庭聚会，用水仙花和雏菊把房间装饰一新。典型的传统做法是布置假环境，可以把房间布置得像过圣诞节一样．也可以布置得像过新年一样，待客人来时，则祝贺他们“圣诞快乐”或“新年快乐”，令人感到别致有趣。

扩展阅读

Trickery On April Fool's Day

Teacher：Boys and girls，there will be an exam tomorrow.

Students：Ah? Really? That's stinks!（讨厌的）

Teacher：Haha，April Fool's! Do you forget what day it is today?

Students：Wow，you were pulling our leg（开玩笑）all along. I was really fooled.

Teacher：Alright，now let's be serious（严肃）. Actually（事实上），you'll take an exam today.

Students：What?

动动手

1. 找找关于愚人节的小故事讲给同学听。
2. 思考：什么样的人是真正的愚人？

Ballet
芭蕾

知识点 To know about ballet
了解芭蕾相关知识

I Feel Like a Bird

Little Jack loves dancing very much and he loves ballet most. He dreams to be a great ballet dancer in the future. So he wants to study ballet in a ballet school in London.

It was Friday, and Jack went to the school with his father. He should do an interview firstly. The teacher asked him many questions about ballet, but Jack did not know any of the answers. His father and the teacher were very disappointed about him. Then the teacher asked the last question, "Why do you love dancing? How do you feel when dancing? "Jack answered, "when dancing, it seems my body is missing. I feel like a bird and I am just flying in the sky."The teacher thought the answer was very good. Jack could enter the ballet school to learn dancing at last.

[**Notes 注释**] **注释**

Words

interview n. 面试　　disappointed a. 失望的

Sentence

His father and the teacher were very disappointed about him. 他的爸爸和老师都非常失望。“Be disappointed about sb.”，“对某人非常失望”，还可用 "be disappointed at” 或 "be disappointed that”，如：He was disappointed at not getting the job. 他因没有得到那份工作而大失所望。还可说 He was disappointed that he didn’t get the job.

[**文章大意**]

轻舞飞扬

小杰克非常喜欢芭蕾舞，梦想到伦敦一所芭蕾学校上学。但在面试中，老师问了很多关于芭蕾的问题杰克都答不上来，这让爸爸和老师都非常失望。最后老师问：“你为什么喜欢跳舞？跳舞的时候是什么感觉呢？” 杰克答道：“跳舞的时候，我觉得自己的身体好像不见了，自己像只小鸟在天空飞翔。”老师觉得这个答案非常好。杰克终于能留下来学习芭蕾舞了。

知识链接

芭蕾起源于意大利，兴盛于法国，“芭蕾”一词本是法语“ballet”的音译，意为“跳”或“跳舞”。它最初是一种人们自娱或在广场上表演的舞蹈。它最大的特点就是演员要穿上特制的足尖鞋立起脚尖跳舞。

扩展阅读

The Origin（起源）of Ballet

Ballet does not appear（出现）suddenly. It takes a long time to develop itself.

In the 16th century，a so-called“court ballet”dance was produced（产 生）in Italy. Actors dressed noble（贵 族的）and elegant（优 雅 的）clothes，and their dance has a soft style. It is also very elegant. This is the original（最初的）form of ballet.

Later，this dance came to France. Moreover（而且），King of France liked dancing very much. It was very popular in France then. Ballet dance teacher and musicians（音乐家）also appeared；They founded the ballet in Paris Dance Academy. In fact，this was the first dance school in the world.

Then，it came to Russia. It also became very popular and developed very well.

动动手

1. TRY TO REMEMBER THESE WORDS. 记一记这些单词。

   Ballet 芭蕾　　interview 面试　　disappointed 失望

   elegant 优雅的　　musicians 音乐家

2. 思考：为什么老师觉得杰克的答案很好？

Christmas
圣诞节

知识点 To know about Christmas
了解圣诞节相关知识

Christmas Day

Christmas Day, the 25th of December, is the biggest festival celebrated in the Christian countries of the world. Although everyone enjoys Christmas Day, it is particularly enjoyed by children. Every child would get very excited because they know they are going to receive presents.

Small children believe that their presents are brought by Santa Claus.

When small children go to bed on Christmas Eve，they hang a stocking at the end of their beds. Then Santa Claus climbs the chimney and puts the presents into children's stockings.

［**Notes 注释**］

Words

festival n. 节日　　particularly adv. 特别是，尤其是

receive v. 收到　　stocking n. 长筒袜　　chimney n. 烟囱

Sentences

Christmas Day，the 25th of December，is the biggest festival celebrated in the Christian countries of the world. 12月25日的圣诞节是全世界基督教国家庆祝的最盛大的节日。"Celebrated"是动词的过去分词，在句中修饰前面的名词"festival"。

When small children go to bed on Christmas Eve，they hang a stocking at the end of their beds. 平安夜孩子们上床时，会把袜子挂在床头。"At the end of"表示"在……末尾"，可以是时间也可是物体，如 We are going on holiday at the end of this month. 我们打算这个月月末去度假。

[文章大意]

圣诞节

12 月 25 日的圣诞节是被世界上基督教国家庆祝的最盛大的节日。尽管每个人都喜爱圣诞节，但最爱圣诞节的还是兴奋的孩子们。因为孩子们知道他们将会在那天收到礼物。

小孩们相信他们的礼物是圣诞老人送的。平安夜孩子们上床时，会把袜子挂在床端。圣诞老人就会从烟囱爬到屋内，把圣诞礼物装进他们的袜子里。

知识链接

圣诞的颜色是红、绿、白三种，圣诞节来临时家家户户都要用圣诞色来装饰。红色的有圣诞花和圣诞蜡烛。绿色的是圣诞树。它是圣诞节的主要装饰品，用砍伐来的杉、柏一类呈塔形的常青树装饰而成。上面悬挂着五颜六色的彩灯、礼物和纸花，还点燃着圣诞蜡烛。

扩展阅读

Postcards from Last Year

It was two weeks before Christmas, and Mrs Smith was very busy. She bought a lot of Christmas Cards and put them on the table in the living room. When her husband came home from work, she said to him, "Here are the Christmas Cards for our friends, and here are some stamps, a pen and our book of address. Will you please write the cards while I am cooking the dinner?"

Mr Smith did not say anything, but walked out of the living room and went to his study. Mrs Smith was very angry, but did not say anything either.

Then a minute later he came back with a box full of Christmas Cards. All of them had addresses and stamps on them.

"These are from last year," he said, "I forgot to post them."

动动手

1. 唱一唱：

Silent Night

Silent night, holy night
All is calm, all is bright
Round young Virgin Mother and Child
Holy Infant, so tender and mild
Sleep in heavenly peace
Sleep in heavenly peace

2. 思考：圣诞节和中国的春节有哪些不同？

Grimm's Fairy Tales
格林童话

知识点 To know about Grimm's Fairy Tales
了解格林童话

Folktale

A folktale is a very old story that tries to explain or understand the world. Such stories were passed down from one generation to another. The stories usually take place long ago in a faraway place and are woven around animals, plants, royalty, or mythical creatures.

In a folktale, goodness is always rewarded. Heroes and heroines live happily ever after while villains are suitably punished. Throughout the generations, the story may change but its core remains the same. Folktales usually have no identified author, but they mirror the values and culture of the society.

Before the Internet, newspapers, radio, television, and other types of media, the world relied on storytellers for entertainment and education. And telling folktales around a fire or hearth was a way for families to spend time together, much in the way that families in our time play family games or watch movies together.

[**Notes 注释**]

Words

folktale n. 民间传说　　explain v. 解释　　understand v. 理解

pass down 流传　　generation n. 一代　　storyteller n. 讲故事的人

mythical adj. 神话的　　rely on 依赖；依靠　　royalty n. 皇室

Sentences

A folktale is a very old story that tries to explain or understand the world. 民间传说是很古老的故事，体现了古代人对世界的解释和理解。“that...”这个关系代词引导定语从句，指“old story”，其还可指“人”，如 He is a man that is never unhappy. 他是一个从来没有不开心的人。

Before the Internet，newspapers，radio，television，and other types of media，the world relied on storytellers for entertainment and education. 在网络、报刊、电视以及其他媒体出现之前，民间传说是主要的娱乐和教育方式。“rely on...”为英语中的固定搭配，意思是“依靠；依赖”，如 We cannot always rely on our feelings. 我们不能总是依靠感觉。

[文章大意]

民间传说

民间传说是很古老的故事，体现了古代人对世界的理解，并一代一代流传下来。这些故事通常都发生在很早很早以前，很远很远的地方。故事基本围绕动物、植物、王室或神话人物展开。

在民间传说中都是好人得到好报，坏人得到惩罚，公主和王子从此幸福地生活在一起。传说的故事情节可能会随着时间的流逝而改变，但故事的核心精神是一致的。民间传说的作者很难确定，但这些故事都映射出其社会特有的价值观和文化。

在网络、报刊、电视以及其他媒体出现之前，民间传说是主要的娱乐

和教育方式。一家人围着火炉讲故事就像我们现在一家人围在一起做游戏或看电视一样，是家人共处的方式。

知识链接

格林童话共有200多篇故事，最有名的包括灰姑娘、青蛙王子、白雪公主、小红帽、睡美人、大拇指汤姆等等。

扩展阅读

Grimm's Fairy Tales

Have you ever worried that Sleeping Beauty（睡美人）would never wake up? Have you hoped to get a pair of Cinderella's（灰姑娘）shoes? Are you happy to see that the hunter saved the Little Red-riding Hood（小红帽）from the wolf's stomach? How interesting stories are，right? Then where do these stories come from? Yes，they are all from Grimm's Fairy Tales.

In Germany，there lived two brothers，the Grimm brothers. They collected tales. We know these stories as "Grimm's Fairy Tales." Many of these tales were told about the countries near Germany，and some of them were partly true.

The Grimm brothers did not really write the stories for boys and girls. They planned them for older people living in Germany. However，when the children heard the stories，they wanted to hear them again and again.

All of this happened long，long ago，but boys and girls everywhere still read and enjoy Grimm's tales.

动动手

1. 你还知道哪些著名的世界童话呢？
2. 思考：童话和现实世界总是有差别吗？你对此有什么看法呢？

Mother’s and Father’s Day
母亲节和父亲节

知识点 To know about Mother’s and Father’s Day
了解母亲节父亲节的由来

Mother’s Day

The first celebration of Mother’s Day can be traced back to ancient Greeks. It is to honor Rhea, the mother of the gods.

In 1907, Anna M. Jarvis, a Philadelphia school teacher, began a movement to set up a national Mother’s Day in honor of her mother, Ann Maria Reeves Jarvis. She asked for help for hundreds of legislators and businessmen to create a special day to honor mothers. The first Mother’s Day was held in a church honoring Anna’s mother. Anna handed out her mother’s favorite white carnations. Anna’s hard work finally paid off in the year 1914, when President Woodrow Wilson set the second Sunday in May as a national holiday in honor of mothers.

[**Notes 注释**]

Words

celebration n. 庆典　　be traced back 追溯到

ancient Greeks 古希腊　　Philadelphia n. 费城

movement n. 运动　　legislator n. 立法者

carnation n. 康乃馨　　pay off 偿还 / 得到回报

Sentences

The first celebration of Mother's Day can be traced back to ancient Greeks. 第一次母亲节的庆典可以追溯到古希腊时期。"be traced back" 意思是“可追溯到”，如 The history of his family can be traced back to 300 years ago. 他们家族的历史可追溯到 300 年前。

In 1907, Anna M. Jarvis, a Philadelphia school teacher, began a movement to set up a national Mother's Day in honor of her mother, Ann Maria Reeves Jarvis. 1907 年，一位费城教师，安娜·米·贾维斯创立了一个在全国范围内纪念母亲的节日，安·米·里弗斯·贾维斯荣誉日。“begin a movement” 意思是“发起运动”，如 It was the school master that began a movement to collect money for poor children. 是校长发起了向贫困儿童捐款的运动。

［文章大意］

母亲节

第一次母亲节的庆典可以追溯到古希腊时期，那时人们举行庆祝活动纪念瑞亚。

1907 年，一位费城教师安娜·米·贾维斯创立了一个在全国范围内纪念母亲的节日，安·米·里弗斯·贾维斯荣誉日。她征集了数以百计的立法者和商业人士一起来创立一个特殊的日子来纪念母亲。第一个母亲节是在一个教堂为安娜母亲举办的。安娜在仪式上发放了她母亲最喜爱的白色康乃馨。安娜的努力终于在1914年得到了回报，时任总统的伍德罗·威尔逊宣布将五月的第二个星期天作为母亲节。

知识链接

康乃馨是母亲节的象征。那是因为安娜·贾维斯在1908年母亲节第一次庆典上将500朵白色康乃馨分送给母亲们。自此以后，每逢母亲节，人们都会送康乃馨。白色的康乃馨是送给已过世的母亲，而红色的康乃馨则送给健在的母亲。父亲节的送花习俗与母亲节相同，只是康乃馨换成了玫瑰。

扩展阅读

Origin of Father's Day

Mrs. John B Dodd, in Washington, is the first one who has the idea of a "father's day". Mrs. Dodd was born on a rural farm in eastern Washington State. When she was a little girl, her mother died when giving birth to the sixth child. His father, William Smart, raised the newborn and other five children by himself. When Mrs. Dodd grew up and had her own baby, she deeply felt that it is very difficult for her father to bring up children.

When first heard a Mother's Day sermon in 1909, she thought of the idea for Father's Day. After many attempts, it was in 1966 that President Lyndon Johnson officially declared the 3rd Sunday of June as Father's Day.

动动手

1. 收集英汉双语母亲节父亲节祝福语。
2. 思考：你知道你爸爸妈妈最喜欢的节日礼物是什么吗？

Sandwich
三明治

知识点 To know the origin of sandwich
了解三明治名字的来历

Fish Sandwich

It was a small factory, and there was nowhere for dinner near it. So the workmen took food from their homes and ate it in the factory at midday.

One of the workmen always had fish sandwiches. Every day he took one of them out of his bag, bit it, and then threw all the sandwiches angrily away.

At last, one day, one of the workmen said to him, "Bill, don't you like fish sandwiches?"

"No," said Bill, "I hate them."

"Then why does your wife make them for you every day? There are lots of other nice things for sandwiches. Tell your wife, and she will make other sandwiches."

"It isn't as easy as that," answered Bill, "I haven't got a wife. I make the sandwiches myself."

[Notes 注释]

Words

nowhere n. 无处、任何地方　　workman n. 工人　　at midday 在正午

fish sandwich 鱼肉三明治　　make sth. oneself 自己做

Sentences

Every day he took one of them out of his bag，bit it，and then threw all the sandwiches angrily away. 每天他都从包里掏出一个三明治，咬一口，然后气冲冲地扔掉。“take sth. out of ...”把某物从……中拿出来，“throw away”扔掉、丢弃。

It isn’t as easy as that. 事情没你说的那么简单。“as easy as…”意思是“和……一样简单、容易”；“that”指代前面的人说的话。“as…as”意思是“和……一样”，表示同级的比较。比如 This book is as interesting as that one. 这本书和那本书一样有趣。

[文章大意]

鱼肉三明治

一个小工厂附近没有吃饭的地方，工人们只能从家里带饭中午在工厂吃。

有一个工人总是带鱼肉三明治。每天他都从包里掏出三明治，咬一口，然后气冲冲地扔掉。

终于有一天，有个工友问他：“比尔，难道你不喜欢鱼肉三明治？”

“是啊，”比尔说，“我讨厌死鱼肉三明治了。”

“那为什么你妻子还天天给你做？可做三明治的好东西多着了！告诉你妻子，让她给你做其他口味的。”

“事情没你说得那么简单，”比尔回答道，“我没有妻子，每天我都自己做。”

知识链接

你知道怎样做三明治吗？准备两片全麦面包，几片火腿，一些生菜和番茄，还要一些奶酪。首先把奶酪涂到一片面包上，然后在面包片上依次铺上生菜、番茄、火腿。最后再把另一片面包盖上。一个三明治就大功告成了。

扩展阅读

How Does Sandwich Get Its Name

We all know what a sandwich is. It is two pieces of bread with ham（火腿）, cheese（奶酪）, and vegetables between them. You can even put anything you like between two pieces of bread to make a sandwich. It is easy to make and so popular with modern busy people. In fact, the man who invented the sandwich was also busy, though he was not busy working, but busy playing cards.

Earl of Sandwich was an Englishman. He liked gambling（赌 博）and hung around all day in the table. One day, he was in a club playing again. Though hungry, he did not want to leave the table to have a meal. His wife brought him some bread and meat, vegetables. Earl of Sandwich put the meat and vegetables in bread. Then he could hold the bread in one hand while playing cards with the other hand. As it was convenient（方 便）, other players also ate this kind of food and called it sandwich.

动动手

1. 试着自己做一个三明治吧！
2. 思考：你认同三明治名字的来历吗？

The Louvre
卢浮宫

知识点 To know about The Louvre
了解卢浮宫

The Louvre

The Louvre is one of the greatest museums in the world, holding the rich artistic heritage of the French people from the early Capetian Kings through the Empire of Napoleon Bonaparte and to the present day.

The Louvre attracts millions of visitors every year from all over the

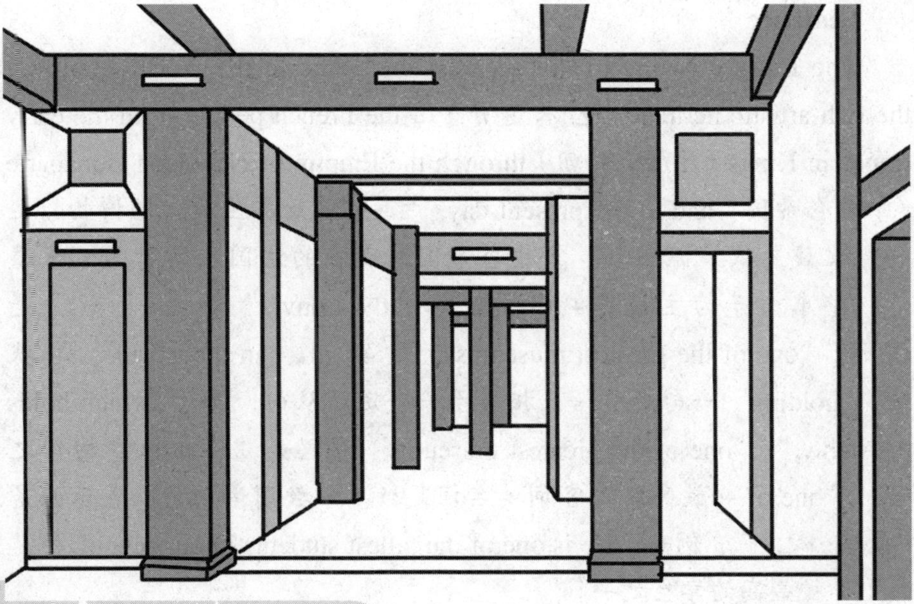

world, with the best art collection anywhere. Among the thousands of priceless paintings is *Mona Lisa*, perhaps the most famous painting in the world. Works of artists like Leonardo da Vinci, David and Titian can also be seen. Among the well-known statues in the collections are *the Winged Victory of Samothrace* and *the Venus de Milo*.

Besides art, The Louvre has many other types of exhibits, including archeology, history and architecture. It has a large furniture collection, with its most grand furniture being *the Bureau du Roi*（法语：国王办公室）of the 18th century.

[**Notes 注释**]

Words

museum n. 博物馆　　artistic heritage n. 艺术遗产

millions of 成千上万的　　priceless adj. 无价　　architecture n. 建筑

Napoleon Bonaparte n. 拿破仑·波拿巴（法国皇帝）的

all over the world adv. 全世界　　archeology n. 考古

Sentence

The Louvre is one of the greatest museums in the world, holding the rich artistic heritage（艺术遗产）of the French people from the early Capetian Kings（卡佩王朝）through the Empire of Napoleon Bonaparte（拿破仑帝国）and to the present day. 卢浮宫是世界上最大的博物馆之一，收藏着从卡佩王朝、拿破仑帝国到现在的法国人所有的艺术遗产。整个句子为主谓宾+补语结构。“the Louvre”是主语，“is”是谓语，“one of the greatest museums”是宾语，“in the world”是状语，“holding”一句是补语，相当于一个定语从句，等于"which holds the rich…"。“one of the greatest museums”意思是“最大的博物馆之一”，“one of + 最高级形容词 + 名词复数 + 单数谓语动词”表示的是“最……之一”，例如，He is one of the tallest students in our school. 他是我们学校最高的学生之一。

[文章大意]

卢浮宫

卢浮宫是世界上最大的博物馆之一，收藏着从卡佩王朝、拿破仑帝国到现在的法国人所有的艺术遗产。

卢浮宫每年吸引世界各地几百万游客，可以说，它拥有世界上最好的艺术收藏。在成千上万无价的绘画作品中有《蒙娜丽莎》——世界上最有名的绘画。这里还可以看到达芬奇、大卫、提香等诸多艺术家的作品。在著名的雕塑收藏品中有《萨莫特拉斯的胜利女神》和《米罗的维纳斯》。

除了艺术品外，卢浮宫还有许多其他类型的展览，包括考古、历史和建筑。它还收藏了很多家具，其中最壮观的是18世纪的国王办公室。

知识链接

卢浮宫是世界上最古老、最大、最著名的博物馆之一。位于法国巴黎市中心的塞纳河北岸，始建于1204年。在卢浮宫里面，有三件价值连城的传世之宝。分别是《爱神维纳斯雕像》、《胜利女神像》和达芬奇的《蒙娜丽莎》。这三件宝贝被称为“卢浮宫三宝”。

扩展阅读

Romantic Paris

A：Which city impressed you most during your trip?

B：It was Paris，I suppose.

A：The name of the city sounds very romantic.

B：Yes，the Eiffel Tower is the symbol of the city. Hard to imagine how it was built over hundred years ago.

A：Did you get to the Louvre Palace?

B：How could I miss it! I spent a whole day inside and still couldn't finish seeing all its collections of world-famous treasures（珍宝）.

A：What treasures?

B：You must have heard about *Mona Lisa*，haven't you?

A：Yes，of course. Did you see the painting?

B：Yes.

A：I'd like to go to Paris at once.

动动手

1. 读一读：法国食物

Fish Roll 鱼卷

Braised Potato 烩土豆

Fried Pig Chop 煎猪排

Spiced Snails 五香蜗牛

Goose Liver Jam 柳橙法国鹅肝酱

2. 思考：对比一下卢浮宫和故宫。

第6章

Health

崇尚健康

Body Part
身体部位

知识点 To know the function of different parts of body
了解身体不同部位的功能

Right Hand or Left Hand

Which of your hands do you use most? Very few of us use both of our hands well. Most of us are right-handed. Only about five people out of a hundred are left-handed. Newly-born（新出生的）babies can take things with either of their hands，but in about two years they like to use their right hands. Scientists do not know why this happens. They have studied this a great deal. They think our animal ancestors were right-handed，but this may not be true. Monkeys are our closest relations in the animal world. Scientists have found that monkeys like to use one of their hands more than the other，but it can be either hand. Next time you visit the zoo，watch the monkeys carefully. You'll see that some of them will swing from their right hand and others will use their left hands.

[**Notes 注释**]

Words

right-handed adj. 惯用右手的（反义词 left-handed）　　ancestor n. 祖先

relation n. 亲戚（同义词 relative）

swing v. 摇荡（还可做名词，表"秋千"）

Sentences

Only about five people out of a hundred are left-handed. 只有 5% 左右的人是左撇子。5% 可用 "five out of a hundred" 来表达，还可用 "five percent" 表达。

"Newly-born babies can take things with either of their hands" "新生儿随便用哪只手都能拿起东西"，和 "...but it can be either hand" "但这可能是左手也可能是右手" 两句中都出现了 "either" 一词，表示 "两者当中的任何一个"，做代词时后面要用 "of"（见前句），做限定词时后面直接跟被修饰的名词（见后句）。"either" 做主语时后面的谓语动词一般为单数，如 Does either of you speak Chinese? 你们两人中有会讲汉语的吗？

[**文章大意**]

习惯左手还是右手？

几乎没人能两只手都用得好。大多数人习惯用右手，只有 5% 左右的人是左撇子。新生儿随便用哪只手都能拿起东西，但大约两年后就会习惯于用右手。科学家不知道这其中的奥秘，他们做了大量研究。他们设想我们的动物祖先是右撇子，但事实未必如此。科学家研究发现和人类关系最近的猴子也是一只手比另一只手用得多，但这只手可能是右手也可能是左手。

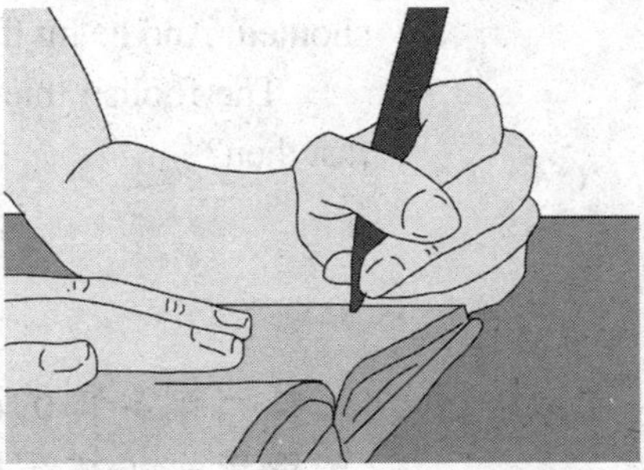

知识链接

眉毛能保护眼睛。每当人们因为热而汗流满面时，眉毛可以阻止额头上的汗水流进眼睛，免得使视线模糊。浓密的眉毛能遮住光线，保护眼睛。眉毛还可以保护多骨的额头遭猛烈的撞击。人们的喜怒哀乐，各种感情无不流露在眉毛上。

扩展阅读

A Foolish Thief

Once upon a time，there was a very foolish thief. He wanted to steal the bell on his neighbour's door. He walked up to the door，took hold of the bell and pulled hard. The bell made a very loud noise. The thief was very frightened（害怕的）and ran home. Then he sat to think，"I must do something about the noise." He thought and thought and at last he had an idea. "Ah，I'll put some cotton（棉 花）in my ears. Then I won't be able to hear the noise."

The next day he went to the door again and took hold of the bell. This time he pulled even harder. The bell rang loudly, but the thief did not hear anything. With another hard pull he got the bell out. Just then his neighbor came running out. "Steal my bell? I'll teach you a lesson（教 训）!" the angry man shouted. And he hit the thief on the nose.

The foolish thief still wondered，"Why did he come out just then?"

动动手

1. 画一幅身体的画，标上各个部位的英语名字吧！
2. 思考：（扩展阅读）为什么说这个小偷很笨？

Sports
体育运动

知识点 To know about your favorite sport
了解自己最喜欢的运动

A Football Match

The animals were bored in the forest. Finally, the lion had an idea. 'I know a really exciting game, and humans like playing it. It is called football. I always watch it on TV."

He told it to the rest of the animals and they all became excited about it so they decided to play. They went out to the field and chose up teams and were ready to begin.

However, the centipede came only until they finished the first 45 minutes. The lion asked him angrily, "Where were you during the first half?" "I was busy putting on my shoes." the centipede answered.

[**Notes 注释**]

Words

bored adj. 无聊的　　the rest of 其余的、剩下的　　centipede n. 蜈蚣

choose up teams 择定对阵双方的球员　　first half n. 上半场

Sentences

However，the centipede came only until they finished the first 45 minutes. 可是直到踢到下半场时，蜈蚣才上场。“until” 意思是“直到……时”，例如：I will be working until 6 o’clock. 我将一直工作到 6 点钟。如果“until”的前面有否定词“not”的话，则意思是“直到……才”，例如，We did not get off the bus until it stopped. 直到车停了，我们才下了公交车。

I was busy putting on my shoes. 我忙着穿鞋去了啊 .“be busy（in）doing sth.“意思是“忙于做某事”，“in” 可省略。类似的用法有 "be busy with sth. “(名词)。例如：我正忙着做作业。可以翻译为 I am busy in doing my homework. 或 I am busy doing my homework. 或 I am busy with my homework.

[文章大意]

动物足球赛

动物们在森林里觉得很无聊。狮子突然想到了一个打发时间的点子：“我知道有一种特别刺激的游戏，叫做足球。人类特别喜欢踢足球。我经常在电视上看他们踢足球。”

狮子向其他动物解释了游戏规则，大家都很激动，于是决定也来踢足球。他们来到森林的草地上，组好队，便开始踢球。

可是直到踢到下半场时，蜈蚣才上场。狮子很生气地问他为什么现在才过来，蜈蚣辩解道：“我忙着穿鞋去了啊！”

知识链接

人的一生在于运动，由此可以知道运动对人的身体健康起到关键的作用。经常运动的人可以增强机体免疫力，锻炼心肺功能，减少患癌症、患高血压的概率。同时运动能让人保持健美的身体，使人身心健康，朝气蓬勃。

扩展阅读

What Is Your Favorite Sport

There are many types of sports，usually running，high jump，long jump，discus（铁饼），football，basketball，badminton，table tennis，swimming and so on. What is your favorite sport? Xiaojie interviews（采访）some students. Some says his favorite sport is football；some says it is playing basketball；some says he likes swimming and some students say their favorite sport is running. China has ranked first in the world in table-tennis（乒乓球）and diving（跳水）. And we can win all the medals in all kinds of competitions in these two items. Liu Xiang is "The Asian Flier"（亚洲飞人）because he is the winner of 110 meter hurdles race（110 米栏赛跑）. He proves to the world：we Chinese can win in this item. Though we are just common persons，we can also make our body stronger by doing sports. We can then work for our country.

No matter what sport you like，you should always keep doing exercise. Then you will be healthy and improve（提高）your study.

动动手

1. 为自己制定一张运动时间表。
2. 思考：怎样才算是合理的运动？

Sub-Health
亚健康

知识点 To know what sub-health is and how to prevent it
了解什么是亚健康以及如何防治

What Is Sub-Health

Sub-health is a kind of state between health and sick. When you are in a sub-health state, you should handle it well so that you can be healthy or else you will get some diseases.

The sub-health can be divided into two kinds: One is the physical sub-health. You may feel tired, weak, uncomfortable all the body. But you cannot find out a reason for this and you are not sick in fact.

Second is the psychological sub-health. You may feel tired in mind or cannot think orderly. Meanwhile, you will feel afraid, worried and you may look down upon yourself; also you will be cold to other people and feel lonely and even you may want to kill yourself.

[**Notes 注释**]

Words

sub-health n. 亚健康　　handle v. 处理　　or else 否则、不然

tired adj. 疲倦的　　divide into v. 把……分成　　physical adj. 身体的

psychological adj.（心理的）　　orderly adv. 有秩序地

look down upon v. 看不起　　meanwhile adv. 同时

Sentence

When you are in a sub-health state, you should handle it well so that you can be healthy or else you will get some diseases. 亚健康状态的人，处理得当身体可向健康方面发展，反之则向疾病方向转变。"be in adj. state" 意思是"处于……状态中"，也可以说"be in a state of n."，例如，"in a sub-health state" 也可说"in a state of sub-health"。"get some diseases" 意思是生病，同样的说法还有："fall ill"，"get ill"，"be taken ill"，"get sick"。

[**文章大意**]

亚健康

亚健康是介于健康和疾病之间的一种部分生理功能下降的状态。亚健康主要有两种，第一种是躯体亚健康，主要表现为不明原因或排除疾病原因的体力疲劳、虚弱、周身不适以及其他身体不适等；第二种是心理亚健康，主要表现为不明原因的脑力疲劳、思维紊乱，同时还有恐慌、焦虑、自卑、冷漠、孤独，甚至产生自杀念头等。

知识链接

摆脱亚健康，我们需要做到以下几点：保证合理的膳食和均衡的营养。其中，维生素和矿物质是人体所必需的营养素；调整心理状态并保持积极、乐观；及时调整生活规律，劳逸结合，保证充足睡眠；增加户外体育锻炼活动，每天保证一定运动量。

扩展阅读

Why Will We Fall Into Sub-Health

Many factors can lead to a sub-health state，such as the environmental pollution in our modern life，improper（不合理的）diet（饮食），smoking and drinking too much and all kinds of pressure（压力）from social competitions（竞争）and so on. Among these factors，the improper diet is the commonest one. For example，some people still obey the traditional diet，and they just eat food with low protein（蛋白质）and high energy. Also many people do not think breakfast important，so they always do not have breakfast. The body is in a state of hunger and there is not enough oxygen for the brain to work. Then the endocrine hormone（内分泌激素）cannot work normally. If it becomes worse，people will feel depressed（抑郁），tired；they cannot see things clearly or faint（晕倒）.

动动手

1. 对照文章看一下你自己是不是处于亚健康状态了，要格外小心哟！
2. 思考：身体有亚健康状态，心理呢？

How to Live Longer
怎样才能活得更长

知识点 To know the knowledge linked with age
了解与年龄有关的知识

How to Live Longer

People seem to be living much longer today than they did about 50 years ago. The average lifespan for people has reached 70 to 76 years old. The maximum lifespan of a human is believed to be around 125 years and the oldest known person lived 122 years 5 months and 14 days. Then how can you live longer?

1. Form a good living habit. You’d better not smoke and drink just a little if you have to. You may of course not stay up too late and you should keep doing exercises every week.

2. Keep a reasonable diet. Balance your diet. You may have a little meat every day, such as fish, chicken and lean meat. Have all kinds of fresh vegetables and fruits. They are good for your health. And don’t forget to have milk and beans.

3. Be happy. This is the most important. To be happy can help you live not only longer but also better.

[**Notes 注释**]

Words

average a; n. 平均（的） lifespan n. 寿命 reasonable a. 合理的

diet n. 饮食 balance n; v. 平衡 stay up 熬夜

Sentences

You’d better not smoke. 你最好不要吸烟。“You’d better” = “you had better”. “had better” 意思是“最好”，没有人称和数的变化，多用

于劝告，如：You'd / He'd better drink more water. 你 / 他最好多喝点水。

To be happy can help you live not only longer but also better. 心情愉悦不但让你活得更长，还能让你活得更好。"not only…but（also）…"的意思是"不但……而且……"，用于连接两个并列的成分，如：He can not only sing well but also dance well. 他不但歌唱得好，舞也跳得好。

[文章大意]

长寿的秘诀

人类的平均寿命远远超过 50 年前，已达 70 多岁。人类寿命的极限预期为 125 岁，目前有记录的最长寿的人活了 122 年 5 个月 14 天。那么，人要怎样才能活得更长呢?

1. 养成良好的生活习惯。最好不要抽烟，少喝酒，不要熬夜并且经常锻炼身体。

2. 保持合理的饮食。每天吃一点肉，比如鱼肉、鸡肉和其他瘦肉。多吃各种蔬菜水果，并且不要忘记喝奶，吃豆制品。

3. 保持愉快的心情。这是最重要的。心情愉悦不但让你活得更长，还能让你活得更好。

知识链接

和外国人初次交往时随便问人家的年龄，特别是问女性的年龄是不礼貌（polite）的行为，因为他们认为这是他们的隐私（privacy）。外国人不喜欢被问的事情还包括（include）收入（income）、体重（weight）、宗教信仰（belief）和婚姻（marriage）状况。中国人习惯的问候（greeting）——"到哪儿去"（where are you going）和"吃了吗"也是不受外国人欢迎的。

扩展阅读

I’ll See You at 12

One day, my wife was ill so we took her to the hospital（医院）. She had to stay there for a week. The hospital had a rule that prohibited（禁止）children under 12 from visiting patients（病人）. Our 11 -year -old son seemed to understand, but our six -year -old daughter took the rule very hard. She was so upset（难过）that she did not even say a word on our way home. After we got home, she talked to her mother on the phone. As she said good bye, she tearfully exclaimed（大叫）, “I’ll see you when I’m 12, Mom!”

动动手

1. 将下列句子翻译成英文。

（1）他 12 岁。

（2）他差两个月 12 岁了。

2. 思考：医院的规定是什么意思？

Advantages of Bike Riding
骑自行车的好处

知识点 To know the advantages of riding a bike
了解自行车的好处

Advantages of Bike Riding

Riding a bike has many advantages for us. If you want to travel, it is a very cheap way because you don't have to pay for gas. Besides, it is safer to ride a bike than drive a car.

Bike riding is especially good for health. It is a good exercise. If you go to school by riding a bike instead of driving or taking a bus, you can have a better chance of getting enough exercise every day.

It is also good for our environment. It makes less noise and does not pollute the air. I am glad to ride a bike to school when my school is not very far from my family.

[**Notes 注释**]

Words

advantage n. 好处　　反义词为 disadvantage

environment n. 环境

especially adv. 特别，尤其　　pollute v. 污染

instead of 而不是；相反

Sentence

If you go to school by riding a bike instead of driving or taking a bus, you can have a better chance of getting enough exercise every day. 如果每天骑车去学校而不是开车或者乘坐公共汽车，我们就能得到充足的锻炼。“Instead of”是介词短语用于连接并列成分，表示“而不是、相反、代替”。如：Try to face the problem instead of dodging them. 要面对问题而不是逃避。

[文章大意]

骑自行车好处多多

骑自行车有很多好处。首先是便宜，不用花钱加油，而且比开车更加安全。其次骑车是一项很好的锻炼项目。如果每天骑车去学校而不是开车或者乘坐公共汽车，我们就能得到充足的锻炼。最后还有环保，自行车很少制造噪音，也不会污染空气。如果我的家离学校不远，我就会选择骑自行车上学。

知识链接

自行车的来源

1790年，有个法国人名叫西夫拉克，他特别爱动脑筋，有一天，他站在路边想：路这么窄，行人又那么多，为什么不可以把马车的构造改一改呢？应当把马车顺着切掉一半，四个车轮变成前后两个车轮……他这样一想，回家就动手进行设计。经过反复试验，1791年第一架代步的“木马轮”小车造出来了。这辆最早的自行车是木制的，它的结构比较简单，既没有驱动装置，也没有转向装置，骑车人靠双脚用力蹬地前行，改变方向时也只能下车搬动车子。即使这样，当西夫拉克骑着这辆自行车到公园兜风时，在场的人也都颇为惊异和赞叹。

扩展阅读

I Can Ride a Bike

Mom and Dad bought a little bike for their son—little Tom. Tom was very happy and kept riding the bike around the house. He was very proud（骄傲）of himself. Around the first lap（圈），Tom shouted，“Mom，look! I can ride a bike without my hand！” Around the second lap，Tom shouted again，“Mom，look! I can ride without my feet!” And around the third lap，Tom reported（报告）to his Mom，“Mom，look! My teeth are gone!”

动动手

1. 学学如何骑自行车。
2. 思考：骑自行车还有哪些好处？

Ice Cream
冰淇淋

知识点 To know why we cannot eat too much ice cream
了解为什么冰淇淋不能多吃

Ice Cream, Eat or Not?

Ice cream can cool us down in summer and it is delicious and full of nutrition. Young people like it very much. However, if we eat too much ice cream, it will do great harm to our health. If we just want to feel happy for that moment and keep eating too much ice cream, it will affect our stomach's working. Meanwhile, the appetite will lose and digestion will be hard for us then. Ice cream should not be eaten especially before or after

meals. If we eat it before meals，it will affect our normal eating and we would not get enough nutrition from meals. If we eat it after meals，it will provide good environment for bacterial so that we may be sick in stomach or intestine. And if a child eats too much ice cream，it will affect the blood flowing in his throat，so the child's immunity will decrease，and he is likely to get upper respiratory tract infections.

Therefore，we cannot eat too much ice cream though it is delicious.

[**Notes 注释**]

Words

ice cream 冰淇淋　delicious adj. 美味的　nutrition n. 营养

stomach n. 肚子；胃　appetite n. 食欲　bacterial n. 细菌

intestine n. 肠胃疾病　throat n. 喉咙　immunity n. 抵抗力

upper respiratory tract infections 上呼吸道感染

Sentences

However，if we eat too much ice cream，it will do great harm to our health. 然而不加节制地大量吃，对健康的危害却不可低估。"do harm to"为固定搭配，意思是"对……有害；危害……"，如 Playing too much games will do great harm to our health。过度游戏会危及身体健康。

And if a child eats too much ice cream，it will affect the blood flowing in his throat，so the child's immunity will decrease，and he is likely to get upper respiratory tract infections. 儿童大量吃冰淇淋，可影响咽喉部血液流动，使抵抗力降低，从而引起反复发作的上呼吸道感染。这四个短句由"if，will，so，and"四个词连接成一个长句。应注意英语中的这种连接。

[文章大意]

"罪恶"的冰淇淋

冰淇淋是夏日里的降温食品，而且有一定的营养，美味可口，很受

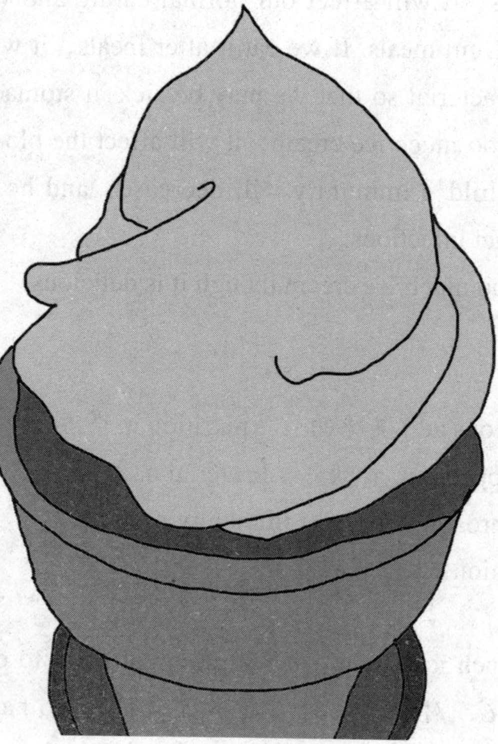

青少年的喜爱。然而不加节制地大量吃，对健康的危害却不可低估。贪图一时痛快，暴饮暴食冰淇淋，可影响胃的功能，导致食欲下降和影响消化。尤其不宜在饭前或饭后吃冰淇淋，饭前吃可影响正常进食，使身体得不到充足的营养；饭后吃则有利于细菌生长，从而导致胃肠疾病。儿童大量吃冰淇淋，可影响咽喉部血液流动，使抵抗力降低，从而引起反复发作的上呼吸道感染。

同时，患有某些疾病者吃冰淇淋也要有所节制，容易引起病情的恶化。

因此，冰淇淋虽然美味，可以吃却不宜多吃。

知识链接

软式冰淇淋\Gelato（意式冰淇淋）是意大利人的发明，并在16世纪由西西里岛的一位教士进行改良，完善了它的制作技术。直到今天，西西里岛的冰淇淋仍被认为是意大利最好的冰淇淋。到过意大利的人们，品尝到意大利冰淇淋，无不为其可口的味道以及精致的外形所惊叹。由于一般是现场制作，冰淇淋就比较软，冰的颗粒也较细，口感也更好。意式冰淇淋是高档冰淇淋的主要代表，而Gelato因为其健康、低卡路里，正日益受到人们的青睐。

扩展阅读

Ice Cream

Ice cream is mainly made of drinking water，milk or milk powder，cream，sugar and so on. We would also put some food additives（食品添加剂）in it，and after some complex process，we can make an ice cream. It has a delicate taste（口感细腻），and it also tastes smooth and cool!

There are many kinds of ice cream and the main nutrition is sugar and fat. Meanwhile（同时），it can provide needed vitamin for our body and help us improve our memory. Ice cream is an important part of the cold drink in summer. People love eating it to be cool.

In all，ice cream can not only help us be cool but also can provide us with some nutrition. So we all love ice cream in summer.

动动手

1. 试着劝朋友少吃冰淇淋并告诉他们少吃的原因。
2. 思考：你能抵得住冰淇淋的诱惑吗？若在生活中面对诱惑时，你应该怎么处理呢？

Overweight
肥胖

知识点 To know the problem of overweight and keep fit
了解肥胖成因和避免超重

There Are Many Fat Children in Chinese Cities

The industry, economy and society develop very fast and this is the main reason for fat problem. There are more and more fat children because people are now living a better life than before, and we see this problem more clearly. In major cities, such as Beijing, Shanghai, Guangzhou, many parents often have no time for cooking because of big pressure in work and life, so their children have to eat fast food for dinner. It is known to us all that fast food can easily make us fat in short time if we eat too much of them, so the children become fat very quickly.

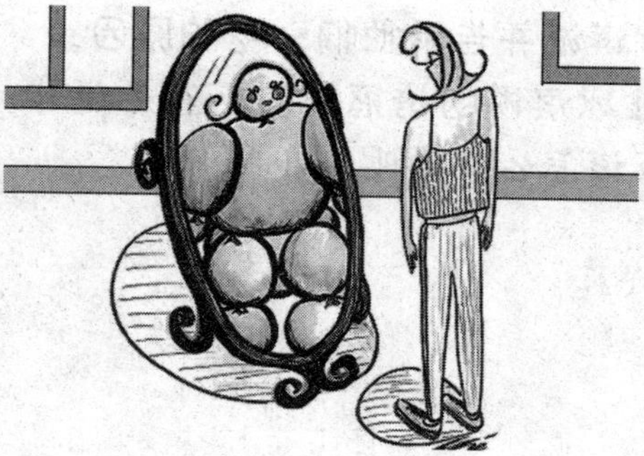

Experts have discussed and studied this problem and tried to find useful methods. We should teach the children about health and nutrition knowledge. At the same time, we should help them to change bad habits, get good diet, and do more exercise to keep fat away. Also it is important to call for parents to spend more time on their children.

[**Notes 注释**]

Words

industry n. 工业　　clearly adv. 清楚地　　pressure n. 压力

easily adv. 容易地　　fast food 快餐　　nutrition n. 营养

Sentences

There are more and more fat children because people are now living a better life than before, and we see this problem more clearly. 人们的生活水平日益提高，儿童肥胖的问题越来越受到关注，人们对它的认识也越来越清晰。"more and more" 意思是"越来越多的"，如 more and more people are using telephones. 越来越多的人使用手机。

Also it is important to call for parents to spend more time on their children. 同时还应倡导父母多关心孩子的身体健康。"it is…to do sth." 为固定搭配句式，即"对某人来说，做某事儿很……"。例如，it is good to take more exercise everyday. 每天多锻炼锻炼身体是很好的事情。

[文章大意]

中国城市里的"小胖墩儿"

随着工业、社会、经济不断向前发展，人们的生活水平日益提高，儿童肥胖的问题越来越受到关注，人们对它的认识也越来越清晰。如在北京、上海、广州这样的大城市中，生活工作压力很大，父母没有时间给小孩做饭吃，于是快餐食品的提供使儿童出现了"小胖墩儿"现象，在这个问题上，专家对引起儿童肥胖的原因及相关克服方法进行了相关讨论和研究。

我们应通过广泛开展健康教育，对儿童进行营养指导，改变不良生活习惯，合理膳食、加强运动，降低儿童肥胖的发生。同时还应倡导父母多关心孩子的身体健康。

知识链接

BMI（Body Mass Index）是指身体质量指数即体质指数，主要用于比较与分析体重对不同高度人健康的影响。BMI是一个中立而可靠的指标，是由19世纪中期比利时的统计学家、数学家和天文学家朗伯·阿道夫·雅克·凯特勒（Lambert Adolphe Jacques Quetelet，1796—1874）最先提出的，它主要是从健康的角度来衡量一个人是否超重或肥胖。BMI是WHO推荐的国际统一使用的肥胖分型标准，其缺点是不能反映局部体脂的分布。通常认为BMI超过24即为超重或肥胖。

BMI计算公式：

BMI = 体重（kg）/ [身高（m）$]^2$

例：某人身高1.65m，体重55kg，BMI = 55/（1.65）^{2} = 20.2

扩展阅读

Fast Food

Fast food is the food that can help people save time and energy，especially for those who keep busy all the time. Why is it called fast food? Because it can be prepared fast and you can buy it fast and you can eat it fast. But because it is too fast, it is not as healthy as those foods we have in too normal way. So，I think we can have the fast food when we are too busy or just when we want something else for change.

动动手

1. 分析一下你自己是否也是“小胖墩儿”呢？
2. 思考：你能抵得住各种美食的诱惑吗？该怎么做才能有效预防肥胖呢？

第7章

Leisure

娱乐人生

Instruments
乐器

知识点 To know about different instruments
了解乐器相关知识

Instruments

There are many musical instruments in Chinese tradition, such as Erhu, Pipa, Yangqin, Guzheng, Dizi, Xiao, Hulusi and so on. These instruments are used for traditional music, classical music, folk music,

and modern music. While in foreign countries, the most popular instruments are sax, piano, violin, guitar, drum and so on. It is very interesting to play any instrument.

[**Notes 注释**]

Words

sax n. 萨克斯　　piano n. 钢琴　　violin n. 小提琴

guitar n. 吉他　　drum n. 架子鼓　　musical instrument 乐器

classical adj. 古典的

Sentence

It is very interesting to play any instrument. 学会演奏某一种乐器是一件非常有趣的事情。"it is...to do..." 意思是"做……很……"，其中it为形式主语，真正的主语为后面的"to do..."，如It is so happy to meet you here. 在这儿碰到你真是太高兴了。

[**文章大意**]

乐器

中国有很多传统乐器，如二胡、琵琶、扬琴、古筝、笛子、箫、葫芦丝等等。这些乐器可用于演奏传统音乐、古典音乐、民间音乐以及现代音乐。然而在国外，比较流行的乐器有萨克斯、钢琴、小提琴、吉他、架子鼓等等。学会演奏某一种乐器是一件非常有趣的事情。

知识链接

作为乐器家族中弦乐器的一员，吉他是一种通过拨动上面一根根的琴弦发出声音的有弦演奏乐器。弹奏时用一只手拨动琴弦，另一只手的手指抵在指板上，指板是覆盖在琴颈上的金属小条。弹奏出来的声音会通过吉他的共鸣箱得到增强。另有一点鲜为人知的是，吉他家族中的“贵族”——古典吉他与小提琴、钢琴并列为世界著名三大乐器。

扩展阅读

Can You Guess?

Once upon a time there was a very rich man and his wife gave birth to three sons! The rich man was going to die soon and his last wish was to let the three sons learn classical instruments（古典乐器）. The rich man liked classical instruments since he was a little boy. He let the eldest son learn the trumpet（喇叭）, the second son learn the flute（笛子）and the third son learn to play the drums（鼓）. Time flied quickly! The three sons had learned how to play their own musical instruments soon. They came back to perform for their father. However, when their father heard the music, he was so angry that he died then. What music did his three sons play? Can you guess?

动动手

1. 记一记乐器名称。
2. 思考：如果你可以学一样乐器，你最想学什么乐器呢？为什么？

Toys
玩具

知识点 To know about kites
了解传统玩具风筝的相关知识

Kite

Kite is one of the toys for ancient Chinese people. Kites were invented by the Chinese people over 2000 years ago. At first, kites were called "Yao", and were also known as "Yuan" in northern part of China. Then how did they get the name of "Fengzheng"?

According to an ancient book, Li Ye, who lived in Five Dynasties, was good at making and flying kites. He tied a whistle made of bamboo to a paper kite. When the wind passed through, the kite made a sound like Guzheng. Since then, a kite that could not make sound was called "Zhiyuan", others were called "Fengzheng". (Feng means wind; Zheng is the musical instrument.) This is how the Chinese name for kite began.

[Notes 注释]

Words

invent v. 发明　flying kites 放风筝　whistle n. 口哨

bamboo n. 竹子　pass through 穿过、通过

musical instrument n. 乐器

Sentence

At first, kites were called "Yao（鹞）", and were also known as "Yuan（鸢）" in northern part of China. 风筝最初被称为"鹞"。在部分北方地区也叫"鸢"。be known as 意思是"被称作"、"被认为"，相似表达有 be known for 意为"因……而著名"，例如：He was known for his honesty. 他以诚实而著称。还有 be known to 意为"为……所知"，例如：He is known to the world because of his books. 他因著作而为世人所知。

[文章大意]

风筝

风筝是古代中国人的玩具之一。中国人2000多年前发明了风筝。风筝最初被称为"鹞"。在部分北方地区也叫"鸢"。那它怎么得名"风筝"的呢？

据古书记载，五代人李邺擅长制作和放风筝。他把一个竹制口哨绑在风筝上，当风吹过，风筝就会发出类似于古筝的声音。由此人们就把不发声的叫

"纸鸢"，能发声的叫"风筝"。这就是风筝名字的由来。

知识链接

芭比娃娃是当今世界销量最大的玩具娃娃，是 1959 年美国妇女露丝·汉德勒为其女儿芭芭拉专门做的玩具。

扩展阅读

Why Was Bob Crying?

Bob is a five-year-old boy. His Dad was going to London on business, so Bob and Mom were seeing Dad off at the airport. After they bought ticket, they sat on the chair to wait for the plane. After a while, Bob suddenly cried aloud. Father was moved and said to Bob, "dear, don't cry. Dad will soon go back and bring you toys." But Bob did not stop crying. Mom smiled and told Dad, "He cried because he saw you paid so much money for the ticket and he was worried that you may have no money to buy him toys."

动动手

1. 你最喜欢什么玩具？能自己动手做一个吗？
2. 思考：现在市面上出现了专门供大人玩的玩具，你怎么看大人玩玩具？

I Love Travelling
我爱旅游

知识点 To know about travelling
了解旅游相关知识

I Love Travelling

I love travelling. Travelling not only helps me to know many things in the world but also makes me happy. What's more, it makes me relaxed. You can go to Disneyland, and there are many things to play. You can certainly be a crazy child there! You can visit one of the "seven wonders of the world," and feel the beauty of nature! You can taste the "magical" ice

water on a glacier，and it can help you become more beautiful and make you live longer.

Just forget all your homework and enjoy your travelling. Experience is also a type of learning. You'll be sure to experience many new things when travelling. You don't even need a tour guide if you want more freedom. Just go with your parents in holidays and don't forget to bring your backpack!

［Notes 注释］

Words

relaxed adj. 放松的、悠闲的　Disneyland n. 迪斯尼乐园

crazy adj. 疯狂的　seven wonders of the world n. 世界七大奇观

magical adj. 魔术的、神奇的　glacier n. 冰川　a type of 一种

tour guide n. 导游　backpack n. 背包

Sentences

travelling not only helps me to know many things in the world but also makes me happy. 旅游不仅帮助我认识了这个世界上很多很多东西，还让我觉得非常快乐。“not only…but also…”是英语中较为常见的一个关联词组，用于连接两个表示并列关系的成分，着重强调后者，其意为“不仅……而且……”；其中的“also”有时可以省略。例如：He works not only on weekdays but on Sundays as well. 他不仅平时工作，星期日也工作。

You'll be sure to experience many new things when travelling. 你绝对能在旅游途中学到很多东西。“be sure to”意思是一定；必定；无疑，同义词有 "must，be bound to do"。

［文章大意］

我喜欢旅游

我爱旅游。旅游不仅帮助我认识了这个世界上很多很多东西，还让我觉得非常快乐。此外，它还让我的心情倍感轻松。你可以去迪斯尼

乐园，那儿有很多东西可以玩，在那儿做一个疯狂的小孩吧！你还可以去参观世界七大奇观，尽情享受大自然的美丽。你还可以品尝冰川上神奇的冰水，据说这可以让你变得更加漂亮，更加长寿呢！

将脑海里所有的作业统统丢掉，尽情在旅游中享受吧！经历也是一种学习。你绝对能在旅游途中学到很多东西。如果你非常渴望自由，那么你甚至不需要导游。你可以在节假日叫上父母一起去旅游，只是要随时记着带着你的背包哟！

知识链接

旅游安全首先应该注意乘车安全。当乘坐汽车、火车或者飞机的时候，我们需要很小心。其次，入住酒店后，我们也应该非常小心。若发现门是坏的，应该找服务员帮你换个房间。再次，对于吃的食物，我们也要很小心。不要随意吃陌生人给的东西。最后，在欣赏美丽风景的时候，应该听从导游的指挥。

扩展阅读

The Great Wall

The Great Wall was listed on the World Heritage List（世界遗产目录）in December 1987.

The Great Wall is located in the north of China. It starts from Shanhaiguan Pass（山海关）in the east and ends at Jiayuguan Pass（嘉峪关）in the west. It is about 6,700 km long. So in Chinese we call it "Wan Li Chang Cheng", and it means Ten-Thousand-li Long Wall（万里长城）.

It was first built during the Spring and Autumn Period（春秋时期）, and then it was built in the Warring States Period（战国时期）more than 2,000 years ago. In order to build the Great Wall, Emperor Qin Shi Huang asked 300 thousand people to work. And it was still built in Han and Ming dynasties（汉朝和明朝）.

The Badaling Section（八达岭长城）is the best place for us to see the Great Wall. In all, the Great Wall is one of the Seven Wonders of the World and a symbol（象征）of the Chinese nation.

动动手

1. 你最想去哪儿旅游呢？
2. 思考：怎样做一个文明的游客？

Dog
狗

知识点 To know more about people's best friend—dogs
了解人类最好的朋友——狗

A Guide Dog

A guide dog is a dog especially trained to guide a blind person. A guide dog must be clever and can follow the owner's orders.

At the age of fourteen months, a guide dog begins a training that lasts three to five months. The dog learns to watch the traffic and to cross the street safely. It also learns to obey such order as "forward", "left", "right"

and "sit" and to disobey any order that might lead its owner into danger.

The most important part of the training is a four-week program in which the dog and its future owner learn to work together. But many blind people are unsuited to work with dogs. Only a tenth of the blind find a guide dog useful.

[**Notes 注释**]

Words

guide dog n. 导盲犬　　especially adv. 特别；尤其；专门

guide v. 引导；带领　　follow the owner's orders 听从主人的命令

unsuited adj. 不合适的　　blind adj. 瞎的

Sentences

A guide dog is a dog especially trained to guide a blind person. 导盲犬是专门为盲人做向导的狗。"be especially trained" 意思是"专门训练"，如 The slaves are especially trained to do this work. 奴隶们专门被训练来干这种活。

The most important part of the training is a four-week program in which the dog and its future owner learn to work together. 训练课程中最重要的部分是4个星期的专门课程。在这个课程中，导盲犬和它未来的主人要学会一同共事。"in which" 此处为一个定语从句，修饰 "a four-week program"，如 we are in a world in which we have to compete each other. 我们处在一个处处与人相争的世界。

[**文章大意**]

导盲犬

导盲犬是专门为盲人做向导的狗。选来接受这种训练的狗必须有很好的脾气、智力、体格和责任心。

在14个月大的时候，导盲犬就开始接受为期3到5个月的训练课

程。导盲犬要学习观望交通情况并能安全穿越街道。它还要学习服从“向前”、“向左”、“向右”及“坐下”等命令，同时学习拒绝服从有可能给主人带来危险的任何命令。

训练课程中最重要的部分是4个星期的专门课程。在这个课程中，导盲犬和它未来的主人要学会一同共事。然而，许多盲人无法适应与狗共事。只有十分之一的盲人觉得导盲犬能帮上忙。

知识链接

Expressions about dog　有关狗的习惯表达

1. Every dog has his own days.　每个人都有自己风光的时候。
2. Love me，love my dog.　爱屋及乌。
3. Barking dogs seldom bite.　爱叫的狗不咬人。
4. You cannot teach old dogs new tricks.　老狗学不了新把戏（老年人很难适应新事物）。
5. Let sleeping dogs lie.　别多事/别惹麻烦。
6. In dog days　夏天的酷热时期
7. a lucky dog　幸运儿
8. a lazy dog　懒汉
9. to lead a dog's life　过着穷困潦倒的生活
10. to rain cats and dogs　（下）倾盆大雨

扩展阅读

Dog Property Rules

1. If I like it, it's mine.
2. If it's in my mouth, it's mine.
3. If I can take it from you, it's mine.
4. If I had it a little while ago, it's mine.
5. If I'm chewing something up, all the pieces are mine.
6. If it's mine, it must never appear to be yours anyway.
7. If it just looks like mine, it's mine.
8. If I saw it first, it's mine.
9. If you are playing with something and you put it down, it becomes mine.
10. If it's broken, it's yours.

动动手

1. 谈谈你喜欢或讨厌狗狗的理由。
2. 思考：狗的财产规则给了你什么启示呢？

Types of Family
家庭类型

知识点 To know about types of family
了解家庭类型

Types of Family

There are several types of family. Nuclear family usually includes parents and children. If your grandparents live together with you, then you get an extended family. If there are no kids, the family would be called DINK (double income, no kids). And of course, there is also single-parent family and blended family for different reasons. Whatever the type is, family means "father and mother I love you."

[**Notes 注释**]

Words

nuclear family 核心家庭　　extended family 大家庭

double adj. 双份的　　DINK 丁克家庭　　blended family 混合家庭

Sentence

If there are no kids, the family would be called DINK (double income, no kids). 不要孩子的家庭称为丁克家庭（夫妻两人都挣工资但不要小孩的家庭）。“if…” 为 if 条件从句，意思是“假如……；如果……”，如 If you study hard, you will go to a good university in the future. 如果你现在努力学习，将来就能上好大学。注：DINK 为 “double income no kids” 四个单词的首字母的缩写。

[文章大意]

家庭类型

家庭有几种不同类型。核心家庭通常只有父母和孩子。如果祖父母加进来就构成了大家庭。不要孩子的家庭称为丁克家庭（夫妻两人都挣工资但不要小孩的家庭）。当然还有各种原因造成的单亲家庭和混合家庭。无论家庭是哪种形式，家的核心就是“爸爸妈妈我爱你们”。

知识链接

成为丁克的首要标准是：具有生育能力而选择不生育，除了主动不生育，也可能是主观或者客观原因而被动选择不生育。其次，主观上对自己丁克身份接纳和认可——他们认为丁克是一种生活方式——这是非常重要的因素。而现实生活中，也正是这些认可自己是丁克角色的群体，能够较好坚持自己的选择，并经营与享受自己的丁克生活。

扩展阅读

The Forgetful（健忘的）Husband

Mr. Smart is terribly forgetful. Every year he forgets Mrs. Smart's birthday if no one reminds（提醒）him. This year, Mrs. Smart decided not to remind again. The day passed like any other. Bedtime for the children came, but Mr. Smart still had not said "Happy Birthday" to his wife.

When Mr. Smart went in to check on the children, he said, "They look so peaceful when they are asleep."

"Yes," answered Mrs. Smart, "they all knew that today was their mother's birthday."

"Did you send her a card?" Mr. Smart asked.

动动手

1. 讲讲你们家发生过的趣事吧！
2. 思考：父母吵架时，怎么才能让家庭的气氛变得和谐？

Jigsaw
七巧板

知识点 To know the beginning of jigsaw
了解七巧板的来历

The Jigsaw

The jigsaw is a popular intellectual game with a history of about 235 years. Once you touch it，you'll just not stop playing it because it is of great variety and owns different levels. Nowadays，people can play this classical game on cellphones or electronic dictionaries.

As to personalized puzzle，it is not only a photo，but a story or a memory. Each piece has its own position；just like that each piece of recalls has its own story. You should put it at the right place to enrich it. But it can not be complete if you put it at the wrong place.

You can put your best recall，which maybe the photos of loved one or the most memorable moment，into a jigsaw. It will make a beautiful dream for you.

［**Notes** 注释］

Words

jigsaw 七巧板　　intellectual adj. 智力的　　classical adj. 经典的

electronic dictionary 电子词典　　personalized adj. 个性化的

recall n. 回忆

Sentences

Once you touch it，you'll just not stop playing it because it is of great variety and owns different levels. 它变化多端，难度不一，让人百玩不厌。“it is of +n”，后面跟抽象名词，其中的 n 相当于其所对应的形容词的意思，例如，"It is of great value" 意思是它的价值很高。

You can put your best recall，which maybe the photos of loved one or the most memorable moment，into a jigsaw. 你可以把你记忆中最深的片段，可以是你挚爱的照片，可以是你最难忘的一瞬留念，做成拼图。此处的 "which" 引导的是非限制性定语从句，修饰“best recall”。

[文章大意]

七巧板

拼图游戏是广受欢迎的一种智力游戏，已经有约 235 年的历史了。它变化多端，难度不一，让人百玩不厌。现在很多手机、电子词典上都有这款游戏。

个性化的拼图，拼凑的不仅仅是一张照片，而是一个故事，一段回忆。每一片的单片都有它自己的位置，就像每段回忆都有它的故事，你要将它放在专属的地方，放对了就慢慢丰富起来，放错了就无法完整。

你可以把你记忆中最深的片段，可以是你挚爱的照片，可以是你最难忘的一瞬留念，做成拼图，变成一个美好的梦。

知识链接

宋朝有个叫黄伯思的人，对几何图形很有研究，他热情好客，发明了一种用6张小桌子组成的“宴几”——请客吃饭的小桌子。后来，有人把它改进为7张桌子组成的宴几，可以根据吃饭人数的不同，把桌子拼成不同的形状，比如3人拼成三角形，4人拼成四方形，6人拼成6方形……这样用餐时人人方便，气氛更好。后来，有人把宴几缩小到只有七块板，用它拼图，演变成一种玩具。因为它十分巧妙、好玩，所以人们叫它“七巧板”。

扩展阅读

Advantages of Jigsaw

Jigsaw is a very useful game. It can help exercise your patience, and change you into a more careful and attentive person. Also, it can improve your power of observation and intelligence, etc. Whenever you finish a work of puzzle, you will get a sense of accomplishment, and then you will find that the picture is so beautiful. And you will feel that there is nothing you can not do because you can finish the puzzle which is so difficult.

动动手

1. 试试如何用七巧板拼出不同的图形。
2. 思考：七巧板的拼接藏着什么奥妙呢？

I Don't Want to Walk Home
我不想走路回家

知识点 To know about car—a necessity in modern life
了解现代生活的必需品——汽车

I Don't Want to Walk Home

Tom is a very old man. After dinner, he likes walking in the street. And he goes to bed at seven o'clock.

But tonight, a car stopped at his house. A policeman helps him get out. He tells Tom's wife, "The old man couldn't find his way in the street. He asked me to take him in the car. "

After the policeman leaves there, his wife asks, "Tom, you go to the street every night. But tonight you can't find the way, what's the matter?"

The old man smiles like a child and he says, "I couldn't find my way? I didn't want to walk home."

[**Notes 注释**]

Words

tonight n. 今晚　　stop at 在……处停下　　policeman n. 警察

matter n. 事情、麻烦

Sentences

After dinner, he likes walking in the street. 他喜欢在晚饭后到大街上散步。"like doing sth." 意思是"（经常或习惯地）喜欢做某事"，属于长期性的爱好，例如：She likes singing. 她喜欢唱歌。和它相近的一个词组是"like to do sth." 是"（偶尔或具体地）喜欢做某事"的意思，例如：I like to swim with you today. 今天我喜欢和你一起去游泳。

What's the matter? 你怎么了？这是一句口头禅，意思是"怎么回事/出了什么事/怎么了？"句子后面还可以加"with sb."表示某人怎么了，例如：What's the matter with her? 她出什么事啦？

[**文章大意**]

我不想走路回家

汤姆是一位老人，他喜欢在晚饭后到大街上散步，7点回来睡觉。

但是，今天晚上一辆小汽车停在他家门前，汤姆在一位警察的帮助下走下汽车。警察告诉汤姆的妻子："这位老人在街上迷路了，他让我用汽车送他回来。"

警察走后，他的妻子问他："汤姆，你每天都到那条街上散步，但是今天你迷路了，你怎么了？"

这位老人像孩子般地笑道："我迷路了？我是不想走路回家。"

知识链接

公安部交管局有关资料显示，截至2011年底，全国机动车保有量为2.25亿辆，其中汽车1.06亿辆。截止2012年底，中国汽车保有量达1.25亿辆，中国已正式进入汽车时代。

扩展阅读

A Clever Panda

A little panda picks up a pumpkin and wants to take it home. But the pumpkin is too big. The panda can't take it home.

Suddenly she sees a bear riding a bike toward her. She watches the bike. "I know! I have a good idea." she jumps and shouts happily, "I can roll a pumpkin. It's like a wheel."

So she rolls the pumpkin to her home. When her mother sees the big pumpkin, she is surprised, "Oh, my God! How can you carry it home?" the little panda answers proudly, "I can't lift it, but I can roll it." Her mother smiled and says, "What a clever girl! Use what you heard to do something."

动动手

1. 你每天放学回家是采用哪种交通工具呢？它的好处是什么？
2. 思考：步行的好处有哪些？

第8章

Chicken Soup

心灵鸡汤

The Treasure Father Left
父亲留下的财产

知识点 To know the significance of work
了解劳动的意义

The Treasure Father Left

A very old farmer called his sons to his bedside to talk with them. "Children," he said, "The time has come for me to die. You will find all my treasure hidden in the vineyard."

As soon as the old Man was dead the sons took their spades and began to dig in the vineyard to look for the treasure. They turned the soil over and over, digging deep into the rich, dark earth.

They found no treasure in the earth but they dig the earth well. It was good for the vines, and the vine produced more grapes than ever before. The sons made wine by the grapes and got much money. Finally, they knew what treasure their father left for them.

[**Notes 注释**]

Words

treasure n. 金银财宝　　hide v. 隐藏　　vineyard n. 葡萄园

spade n. 铁锹　　dig into 挖、掘　　earth n. 土　　vine n. 葡萄酒

grape n. 葡萄

Sentence

A very old farmer called his sons to his bedside to talk with them. 一个老农夫把儿子们叫到床前，和他们说话。“talk with sb.”意思是“和某人交谈”，例如：I'd like to talk with you. 我想和你谈谈。相似表达还有“talk to sb.”意为“对某人说话”，例如：He stopped to talk to me when seeing me. 看到我的时候，他停下来和我说话。“talk about”意为“讲、谈论、交谈”，例如：I never talk about gossip. 我从不传播流言蜚语。

[**文章大意**]

父亲留下的财产

一个非常老的农夫把儿子们叫到床前，和他们说话。“孩子们，”他说，“我就要离开人世了，你们在葡萄园里能找到我埋藏的金银财宝。”

老人刚一去世，他的儿子们就拿上铁锹到葡萄地里去挖寻财宝了。他们把土翻了又翻，一直挖到了肥沃的黑土。

他们在地里没有找到金银财宝，但是，土地被铲过之后，种在上面的葡萄长得非常好，比以往产出更多的葡萄。儿子们把这些葡萄酿成葡萄酒卖了很多钱，他们也终于明白了父亲留给他们的财宝是什么。

知识链接

五一国际劳动节简称“五一”节，在每年的5月1日。劳动节源于美国芝加哥的工人大罢工。1886年5月1日，芝加哥的20多万工人为争取实行8小时工作制而举行大罢工，最终获得了胜利。新中国成立后，我国将5月1日定为法定的劳动节。

扩展阅读

The Ox and the Dog

An ox and a dog serve for the same farmer.

One day the dog speaks to the ox with pride，“How grand I am! In the daytime，I watch out for the cattle in the meadows（牧场）；At night，I guard the house. But you…”

“Me? How about me? “the ox wonders.

“You can only plough（犁地）or draw a cart.” the dog slightly says.

“Yes. It’s true,” the ox says. “But if I don’t plough，what do you guard? “

动动手

1. 记一记关于劳动的名言警句。

No pains，no gains.　没有付出就没有收获。

As you sow you shall mow.　种瓜得瓜，种豆得豆。

The early bird catches the worm.　早起的鸟儿有虫吃。

He that will not work shall not eat.　不劳动者不得食。

An hour in the morning is worth two in the evening.

一日之计在于晨。

2. 思考：你怎样理解“NO PAINS, NO GAINS.”这句话？

Dream

梦想

知识点 To know why everyone must have a dream
了解为何人类必须要有梦想

Dream

As to our human beings，a dream is a vision and desire for good things. It is a kind of pursuit and full of power. While many people are talking about dreams，few of them will try to do something to make it true. Even when they actually do something，they will easily give up. At last，the dream is

第8章 心灵鸡汤

still a dream.

Young people always dare to speak out their dreams, but they often forget it after speaking it out. It seems that they are not afraid of being laughed by others. We often hear of someone learning design because he wants to be a clothes designer in the future; or someone is learning translation because he dreams to make a living by it. However, one year later, when you remind them of their dreams, they would just shake the hands and say, "It is not that easy, and I give up earlier." Do they meet any problems? Not yet! They just give up their dreams even before they begin doing something about it.

In fact, dream is the lifelong commitment to ourselves, and we should treat it seriously and try to realize it.

[**Notes 注释**]

Words

pursuit n. 追求　　actually adv. 实际上　　give up 放弃

clothes designer 服装设计师　　translation n. 翻译

lifelong commitment 一生的承诺　　seriously adv. 严肃地

Sentences

While many people are talking about dreams, few of them will try to do something to make it true. 虽然"说"梦想的人多，但"做"梦想的人少。"while"意思是"虽然"，起让步的作用，如 While you are rich, you cannot bully people. 虽然你很有钱，但你也不可以欺负人。

They just give up their dreams even before they begin doing something about it. 其实在还没开始付出之前，他们就自动放弃梦想了。"before"意思是"在……之前"，是一个副词，如 Mom made dinner before I came home. 我回家前妈妈就做好了饭。

[**文章大意**]

梦想

梦想是人类对于美好事物的一种憧憬和渴望，一种意识里的追求和动力的源泉。但事实上，“说”梦想的人多，“做”梦想的人少，很少人有进一步的行动；就算有行动，也很少有人持之以恒，最后梦想还是梦想。

这也是为什么年轻人敢大声说出自己的梦想，因为年轻人说完就忘了，也不怕别人笑。所以我们常听说某某在学设计，希望将来当个服装设计师，或是某某在学翻译，希望能以此作为未来之路。可是再过一年之后，你再提起这个梦想时，他们会摇摇手说：“没那么简单，早就不想了。”那是碰到什么困难了吗？其实连开始都没有，他们就自动放弃了。

其实，梦想是一个人对自己一生的“承诺”，必须严肃认真地面对它、实践它。

承载希望

放飞梦想

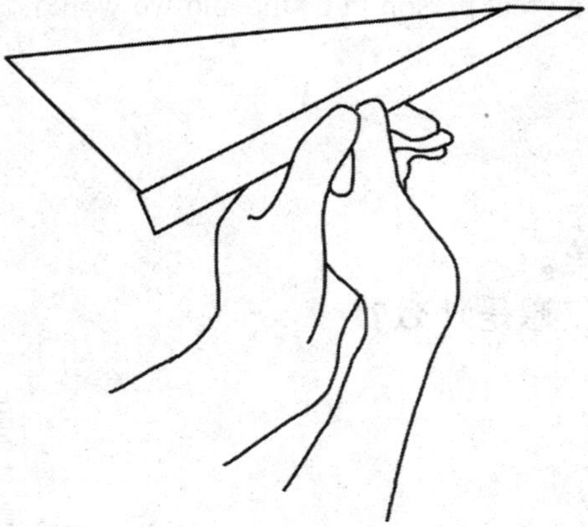

知识链接

《我有一个梦想》(*I have a dream*)是马丁·路德·金于1963年8月28日在华盛顿林肯纪念堂发表的著名演讲，内容主要关于黑人民族平等。对美国甚至世界影响很大，至今还广为流传。

扩展阅读

The Dream of Premier Zhou Enlai

When he was young, Premier Zhou Enlai just dreamed to study for his motherland—China.In 1910, he was twelve and went to a school for study. One day, the teacher asked them, "Why do you come here to study?" Some said, "I want to be a polite person." Some said, "Because I want to make my family proud of me." And some said, "I want to help my father to do the accounting work (记账)." And when it was Zhou's turn, he answered carefully, " I study for the rise of China!" All the students laughed at him. However, he has proved himself by hard work for his dream—the rise of China. And finally, he became a great person in China and we would remember him forever.

动动手

1. 写下你的梦想清单。
2. 思考：你最大的梦想是什么？

Carrot, Egg and Coffee
胡萝卜、鸡蛋和咖啡

知识点 To know how to face a difficulty
了解如何面对困难

Carrot, Egg and Coffee (Ⅰ)

It's a story about carrot, egg and coffee. A daughter complained to her father about her life. She thought things were so hard for her and she didn't know what to do. She was tired of her life. It seemed as one problem was solved and a new one began.

Her father, a cook, took her to the kitchen, and filled three pots with water and put them on a fire. Soon the pots came to a boil. In one he put carrots, in the second he put eggs, and in the last he put coffee beans. He let them boil, without saying a word.

The daughter pouted her lips and impatiently waited, wondering what he was doing. In about twenty minutes he turned off the stoves. He took the carrots out and put them in a bowl，pulled the eggs out and put them a bowl，and then he poured the coffee in a cup. Turning to her and asked，“Darling，what do you see?”

“Carrots，eggs，and coffee.” she replied.

[**Notes 注释**]

Words

complain v. 抱怨　　cook n. 厨师　　kitchen n. 厨房　　pot n. 锅

carrot n. 胡萝卜　　coffee bean 咖啡豆　　boil v. 沸腾

stove n. 炉子　　bowl n. 碗

Sentences

A daughter complained to her father about her life. She thought things were so hard for her and she didn't know what to do. She was tired of her life. 女儿向父亲抱怨她的生活，她觉得凡事都很艰难，不知该怎样办。她厌倦了自己的生活。“complain about”的意思是“抱怨……”，如 She often complain about her job. 她经常抱怨自己的工作。“be tired of”的意思是“对……感到厌倦”，如 I feel tired of him. 我对他感到厌倦。

He let them boil，without saying a word. 他让它们煮沸，一言不发。“without saying a word.”此处做伴随状语，对父亲的状态进行描述。如 She looks at the table，without saying a word. 她盯着桌子，一言不发。

[文章大意]

胡萝卜、鸡蛋和咖啡

女儿向父亲抱怨她的生活，她觉得凡事都很艰难，不知该怎样办。她厌倦了自己的生活，好像问题一波刚平，一波又起。

她的父亲是名厨师，他把她带进了厨房，在三口锅里分别装进了水，然后放到火上烧。很快，锅里的水开了。他一句话也没说，往第一个壶里放了些胡萝卜，往第二个壶里放了鸡蛋，在最后一个里面放了些咖啡豆，让它们煮沸，却不说一句话。

女儿撅着嘴，不耐烦得等着，很纳闷父亲到底想做什么。大约二十

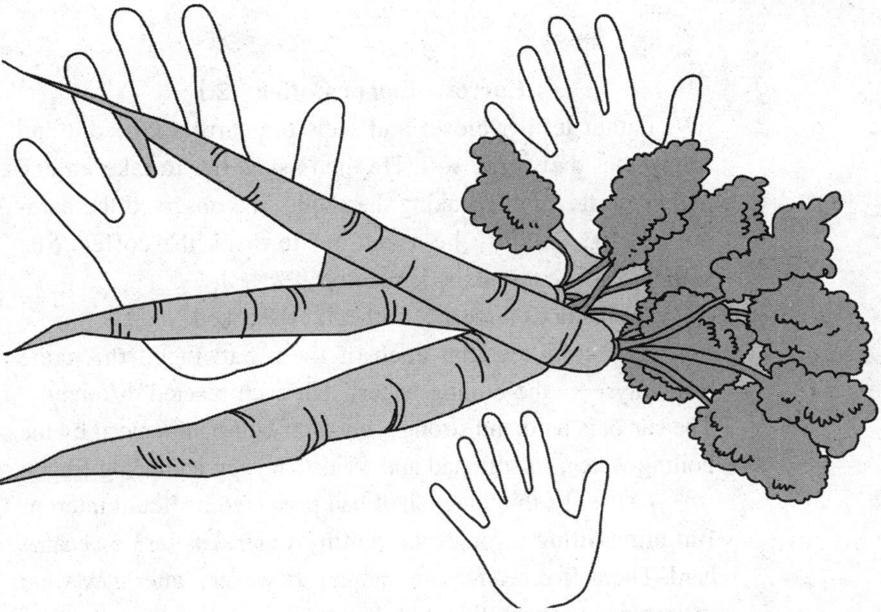

分钟后，父亲关了炉子，把胡萝卜倒进一个碗里，又把鸡蛋拿出来放进另一个碗里，接着把咖啡倒进一个杯子里，然后转过头来，对她说，“亲爱的，你看见了什么？”

“胡萝卜、鸡蛋和咖啡。”她答道。

知识链接

美国姑娘海伦·凯勒在19个月大的时候得了一场怪病，成了聋哑人。不过幸运的是，一位叫安妮·萨利文的人帮助了她，教她用双手说话。萨利文老师让海伦触摸周围的东西，然后用她和海伦都懂得的手语告诉她这叫什么。就这样，海伦克服了困难，重获新生。

扩展阅读

Carrot，Egg or Coffee（2）

Father let her closer and feels the carrots. She did and found that they were soft. He then asked her to take an egg and break it，after breaking the shell，she observed the hard-boiled egg. Finally，he asked her to drink the coffee. She smiled，as she tasted its rich aroma（芳香）.

"What does it mean，Father?" she asked.

He explained that each of them had faced the same difficulty ——the boiling water，but each reacted differently. The carrot is hard and strong，but after being influenced by the boiling water，it softened and weak. The egg had being fragile（易碎的），its thin outer shell had protected its liquid interior. But after sitting through the boiling water，its inside became hard. The coffee beans were unique；however，after they were in the boiling water，they had changed the water.

"Which are you?" he asked his daughter.

When difficulty knocks on your door，how do you respond? Are you a carrot，an egg，or a coffee bean?

动动手

1. 搜集关于挫折的名言警句。
2. 思考：你从文中的小女孩的经历中领悟到了什么道理？

Failure and Success
失败与成功

知识点 To know that failure is the mother of success
了解失败乃成功之母

THE SIGNIFICANCE OF FAILURE

Robert H. Schuller

Failure doesn't mean you are a failure, It does mean you haven't succeeded yet.

Failure doesn't mean you have accomplished nothing, It does mean you have learned something.

Failure doesn't mean you have been a fool, It does mean you had a lot of faith.

Failure doesn't mean you've been disgraced, It does mean you were willing to try.

Failure doesn't mean you don't have it, It does mean you have to do something in a different way.

Failure doesn't mean you are inferior, It does mean you are not perfect.

Failure doesn't mean you've wasted your life, It does mean you have a reason to start afresh.

Failure doesn't mean you should give up, It does mean you must try harder.

Failure doesn't mean you'll never make it, It does mean it will take a little longer.

Failure doesn't mean God has abandoned you, It does mean God has a better idea.

[**Notes 注释**]

Words

failure n. 失败　　succeed v. 成功　　accomplish v. 完成

disgraced adj. 羞辱的　　inferior adj. 差的；下等的

afresh adv. 重新　　abandon v. 抛弃

Sentences

Failure doesn't mean you are a failure; It does mean you haven't succeeded yet. 失败并不代表你是个失败者，它只表明你尚未成功。此处的 "does" 无实际意义，只是起强调作用，如 She does want to see you. 她真的很想见你。

Failure doesn't mean God has abandoned you; It does mean God has a better idea. 失败不代表上帝已经抛弃你，它只表明上帝还有更好的主意。这两句话均为宾语从句，"mean" 后面省略了 "that"，如 It means (that) you can have a better life. 这意味着你可以过更好的生活。

[**文章大意**]

失败的意义

罗伯特·舒勒著　陈采霞译

失败并不代表你是个失败者，它只表明你尚未成功。

失败并不代表你一无所获，它只表明你吸取了一次教训。

失败并不代表你很愚蠢，它只表明你信心百倍。

失败并不代表你无脸见人，它只表明你百折不回。

失败并不代表你工夫白费，它只表明你的做事方法尚待改进。

失败并不代表你低人一等，它只表明你并非完人。

失败并不代表你浪费生命，它只表明你有理由重新开始。

失败并不代表你应该放弃，它只表明你要加倍努力。

失败并不代表成功永不属于你，它只表明你要付出更多的时间。

失败并不代表上帝已经抛弃你，它只表明上帝还有更好的主意。

知识链接

Proverbs about Success

1. Failure is the mother of success. 失败乃成功之母。

2. Success is 99% perspiration and 1% inspiration. 成功是 99% 的汗水和 1% 的灵感。

3. Four short words sum up what has lifted most successful individuals above the crowd：a little bit more. 成功的秘诀就是四个简单的字：多一点点。

4. You have to believe in yourself. That's the secret of success.（Charles Chaplin，American actor）人必须相信自己，这是成功的秘诀。（卓别林，美国演员）

5. If you wish to succeed，you should use persistence as your good friend，experience as your reference，prudence as your brother and hope as your sentry.（Thomas Edison，American inventor）如果你希望成功，当以恒心为良友、以经验为参谋、以谨慎为兄弟、以希望为哨兵。（爱迪生，美国发明家）

扩展阅读

Mr. Going-to-do

The Browns are our neighbor. Mr. Brown's first name is John. But when his neighbors are talking about him, they all call him "Mr. Going-to-do." Do you know why? Mr. Brown always says he is going to do something, but he never does it.

Every Saturday Mr. Brown goes to Mr. Smith's backdoor and makes some talks to him. He always says he is going to do something. "I'm going to clean my home today." Or "I'm going to wash my car tomorrow," or "These trees in front of my house are too big. I'm going to cut them down next week."

Mr. Smith usually says, "are you, John?" He knows his neighbor is not going to clean his house, or wash his car, or cut down the trees. Then he says, "Well, sorry John, I'm going to do some work in the house." And he leaves.

Mr. and Mrs. Smith often say to their son Dick, "Are you going to do something? Then do it! Don't be another Mr. Going-to-do!"

动动手

1. 试举出你心目中的成功人士。
2. 思考：最近干的最失败的事情是什么？你是如何调整心态，继续努力的呢？

Friendship
友谊

知识点 To know what real friendship is
了解什么是真正的友谊

The Story of "High Mountain and Running Water"

During the Spring and Autumn period，there was a famous man named Yu Boya. He was good at playing the Guqin（a kind of musical instrument）.

One day，Yu Boya was playing the Guqin in a boat. The music became more and more beautiful when someone on the bank shouted "Great!" . Hearing the shouting，Boya came out of the boat. He saw a woodcutter on the bank. Boya was happy，because the woodcutter understood his music. He invited the woodcutter into his boat and played Guqin for him. When he

played some music about mountains, the woodcutter said, "Wonderful music! I can see Mountain Tai reaching the sky." When Boya played the music about water, the woodcutter said, "Wonderful music! I can see the running waters!" Boya was excited and said, "Friend! You are my real friend!"

That woodcutter was Zhong Ziqi. Since then, they had been good friends. And the words "high mountain and running water (高山流水)" were then used to refer to true friends who understand each other.

[**Notes 注释**]

Words

the Spring and Autumn period 春秋战国时期　　be good at 擅长

musical instrument 乐器　　bank n. 岸上　　shout v. 叫喊

woodcutter n. 樵夫　　refer to 指的是

Sentences

During the Spring and Autumn period, there was a famous man named Yu Boya. 春秋战国时期，有个很有名的音乐家叫俞伯牙。"named"为后置定语，修饰前面的"a famous man"，如 He is my brother named Xuanxuan. 他是我弟弟，名字叫轩轩。

Hearing the shouting, Boya came out of the boat. He saw a woodcutter on the bank. 听到叫声，伯牙走出船舱，看见岸上站着一个樵夫。此处的"hearing..."为现在分词做状语，强调状态，如 Hearing the music, he danced soon. 听到音乐声后，他立马跳起舞来。

[**文章大意**]

高山流水的故事

春秋战国时期，有个很有名的音乐家叫俞伯牙。他擅长弹古琴。

一天，伯牙在船上弹奏古琴。悠扬的琴声飘荡在河上。岸上有人高声叫道："好音乐！"听到叫声，伯牙走出船舱，看见岸上站着一个樵夫。他知道樵夫听得懂他的音乐，非常高兴，便邀请樵夫上船小坐。伯牙抚琴专门为樵夫演奏。当他弹奏起赞美高山的曲调时，樵夫赞叹：“真好！好像

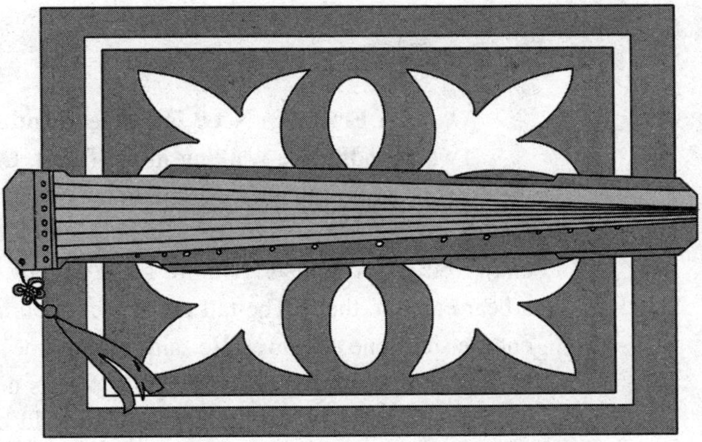

高耸入云的泰山！”当伯牙弹奏表现汹涌波涛的曲调时，樵夫赞叹：“好！好像滚滚奔腾的流水！”伯牙兴奋极了，激动地说：“知音！你真是我的知音！”

那个樵夫就是钟子期。从此二人成了最好的朋友。“高山流水”这个词也流传下来，用来指知心朋友。

知识链接

赠汪伦
李白
李白乘舟将欲行，忽闻岸上踏歌声。
桃花潭水深千尺，不及汪伦送我情。

To Wang Lun
Li Bai
On board and about to set sail,
suddenly I hear you stamping and singing on the shore.
Peach Blossom Spring is a thousand fathoms deep,
but your love for me is deeper as I leave.
（by Tony Barnstone，Willis Barnstone and Chou Ping）

扩展阅读

A Friend in Need Is a Friend Indeed

Two friends were walking in the forest. One is tall, and the other is short. The tall man said to the other, "We are good friends. If any beast comes, I'll help you." The short man answered, "Of course, we are good friends." At this time a bear came to them. The tall man quickly climbed up a tree, but the short one couldn't. He said, "Help me, I can't climb up." But the tall man said, "No, the tree is not strong." The short man had to lie on the ground and held his breath. The bear smelt him and went away. The tall man came down and asked, "What did the bear say to you?" "He runs away from you when you are in great need. He is not your friend," he answered. Remember: A friend in need is a friend indeed.

动动手

1. 你有几个好朋友呢？试着多交几个好朋友吧。
2. 思考：结交朋友最重要的原则是什么呢？

Help
帮助

知识点 To know that to help others is to help yourself
明白帮助他人就是在帮助自己

The Helpful Ant

An ant is walking by the river. He looks at the river and says to himself, "How nice and cool this water looks! I must drink some of it." But when he is drinking, he slips into the river.

"Oh. Help! Help!" The ant cries,

A dove is sitting in the tree. She hears him and throws him a leaf, "Climb up that leaf," she says "And you will float to the bank."

The ant climbs up onto the leaf, and the wind blows the leaf to the bank. And the ant is saved.

"Thank you, Dove. You're so kind," The ant says and runs home, "You have saved my life, and I wish I could do something for you, Goodbye!"

"Goodbye!" says the dove, "Be careful. Not to fall into the river again."

After a few days, the dove is building her nest. And a man is raising his gun to shoot her.

The ant sees this, and runs quickly to bite the man's leg. "Ouch!

Ouch! ” The man feels pained and drops his gun. The dove hears and flies away. So the man picks up his gun and leave.

The dove comes to her nest. “Thank you，my little friend，” she says，“You have saved my life.”

The little ant is so glad，because he can help the dove.

[**Notes 注释**]

Words

ant n. 蚂蚁　　nest n. 巢

Sentences

Be careful. 小心。衍生词组“be careful of ...”，意思是“注意，小心……”后接名词，动名词或从句。例如：Please be careful of your spelling. 注意你的拼写。同义词组还有 "be careful with..." 也是“小心……”的意思。Be careful with the wet paint. 小心，油漆未干。

You have saved my life. 你救了我的命。“have+done”是现在完成时，描述过去发生的而与现在情况有关的事或状态。例如：He has been to the Great Wall twice. 他去过两次长城。

[**文章大意**]

热心助人的蚂蚁

一只蚂蚁在河边散步。他看见喝水自言自语道：“这河水看上去真清凉啊！我要去喝点。”可是他在喝水的时候，一不小心滑进河里了。

“啊！救命！救命！”蚂蚁叫喊着。

一只鸽子正待在树上，听见呼救声，就扔给他一片树叶。“快爬到树叶上去”。她说：“你会漂到岸上的。”

“谢谢你，鸽子。你真善良。”蚂蚁一边说一边向家跑，“你救了我的命，我会报答你的。再见！”

"再见！小心别掉进河里了。"鸽子说。

几天后，鸽子正在筑巢，一个人举着枪要打鸽子。蚂蚁看见了，迅速地跑过去，在那个人的腿上咬了一口。"哎呀！哎呀！"那个人疼得扔掉枪。鸽子听见了，连忙飞走了。那个人只好捡起枪，走了。

鸽子又飞回巢里。"谢谢你，我的小朋友。"鸽子说，"你救了我的命。"

小蚂蚁很高兴，因为他也帮助了鸽子。

知识链接

1985 年 12 月 17 日，第四十届联合国大会通过决议，从 1986 年起，每年的 12 月 5 日为"国际促进经济和社会发展志愿人员日"（International Volunteer Day for Social and Economic Development 简称：国际志愿人员日），其目的是敦促各国政府通过庆祝活动唤起更多的人以志愿者的身份从事社会发展和经济建设事业。

扩展阅读

The Bathing Boy

One day，Tom is bathing in a river. He doesn't swim well and will be drown. He calls out loud for help. A man is just passing by. He doesn't help the boy，but stands by and says to him. "How imprudent you are! It is dangerous to bath in the river." "Oh，yes sir，" cries the boy，"Please help me out and scold me afterward."

Counsel without help is useless.

动动手

1. 学雷锋日是哪一天呢？你在那天做好事了吗？
2. 思考：帮助别人会给你带来什么好处呢？

The Strong in Life
生活中的强者

知识点 To know that everyone can be the strong in life
了解人人都能成为生活中的强者

Who Is the Strongest

Once there was a little ant. She wanted to get married, but she only wanted to marry the strongest creature.

She wanted to marry the strongest creature, but she didn't know who the strongest creature is. She saw the wind blow houses down. So she thought the wind was the strongest creature. She wanted to marry the wind.

But the wind told the little ant that he wasn't the strongest creature. There was a tower in the forest. He had stood there for a thousand years against his force. The tower was the strongest creature.

"Why do you want to marry me?" the tower asked.

"Because you are the strongest creature in the world. You are stronger than the wind." said the mouse.

"You are right. I'm stronger than the wind. But I'm not the strongest creature in the world. Look, how I'm damaged! Can't you guess who has done this to me? It's you, ant."

At last, the little ant married her own kind. They were the strongest creatures.

[**Notes 注释**]

Words

marry v. 结婚　　creature n. 生物　　damaged adj. 被损坏的

Sentences

She saw the wind blow houses down. 她看到风把房子吹倒了。"blow down" 是个词组，意思是“吹倒”，例如：The storm blew down many trees. 这场风暴刮倒了许多树。

Look, how I' m damaged! 瞧，我已被损坏成什么样子了。这个句子是由“How”引导的感叹句，“how”用来修饰形容词、副词或动词。例如：How interesting the story is! 这故事真有趣！

[**文章大意**]

谁最强大

从前，有一个小蚂蚁想结婚，但她只想嫁给世界上最强大者。

她想嫁给最强大者，但她不知道谁才是最强大者。她看到风把房子吹倒了，于是她认为风是最强大的，她要嫁给风。

可风告诉小蚂蚁，他不是最强大者，林中有一座塔。他顶住风力耸立了一千年，他才是最强大的。

“为什么你要嫁给我？”塔说。

“因为你是最强大的，你甚至比风还强大。”蚂蚁说。

“你说的对，我是比风强大。但我不是最强大的。瞧，我已被损坏成什么样子了。难道你猜不出来是谁把我损坏成这个样子的吗？是你们蚂蚁啊。”塔说。

最后，小蚂蚁嫁给了她的同类，因为他们才是最强大者。

知识链接

怎样让自己的内心更强大

一. 从生活细节做起。抬头挺胸走路，想象自己像棵松树一样挺拔；公众场合提高音量，敢于表达自己的想法；每天早晨对镜微笑三分钟，让每天拥有愉悦的心情。

二. 提升文化素养。

三. 自信心培养。敢于承认错误，勇于承担责任；不轻易否定自己，适当坚持自己的观点，并尝试说服别人接纳；面对困难不逃避，及时迎难而上，主动思考解决方法。

四，尝试有始有终做一些不是很难的事，训练自己的毅力及耐力。总的来说不是一朝一夕就能促成，最重要的一条就是相信自己，慢慢地你会发现自己坚强起来的。

扩展阅读

Three Good Friends

One day, a monkey rides his bike near the river. Meanwhile, he sees a lion under a tree running at him. He is afraid and falls into the river. Worstly he can't swim. He shouts for help. The rabbit hears the shouting, so he jumps into the river and swims to the monkey, but he can't help him. Luckily, an elephant comes along. He is very strong. He helps the rabbit and monkey. Three of them are very happy. Afterwards, they go to the elephant's home and become good friends.

动动手

1. 你会通过哪些方式让自己的体魄更强壮呢？
2. 思考：你的内心够强大吗？